Health, Healing and the Holy Spirit

Wendy Creel

TRILOGY CHRISTIAN PUBLISHERS

TUSTIN, CA

Trilogy Christian Publishers
A Wholly Owned Subsidiary of Trinity Broadcasting Network
2442 Michelle Drive
Tustin, CA 92780

For information, address Trilogy Christian Publishing

Rights Department, 2442 Michelle Drive, Tustin, Ca 92780.

Trilogy Christian Publishing/ TBN and colophon are trademarks of Trinity Broadcasting Network.

For information about special discounts for bulk purchases, please contact Trilogy Christian Publishing.

Manufactured in the United States of America

10 9 8 7 6 5 4 3 2 1

Library of Congress Cataloging-in-Publication Data is available.
ISBN 978-1-64773-995-9
ISBN 978-1-64773-996-6 (ebook)

Contents

Dedication

Dedicated to God for with Him all things are possible and without Him none of this would have been possible.

Introduction

As a Naturopathic Doctor and Master Herbalist, I am in a continual search for the many and varied answers to healing. Not just healing the body, but healing the spirit and the emotions. If we believe all else will follow, if we work to remove the stains of sin smeared upon our spirit due to the fall from grace, the fall from God's original plan. God is redemptive and desires to restore all that was lost, but we must become willing participants.

This is my journey from growing up determined to be an atheist, then diving into the New Age movement, and finally into a radical encounter with Jesus Christ Himself.

How interesting God is that He leads you from one revelation to another when you diligently search for the truth. He will use any path you take, as long as you do not camp there but continue searching for the Truth.

This is my personal path of discovery and revelation of truth. It is a supernatural disclosure of the lies that bind us and hold us prisoners: first in our Spirit, then our mind and emotions, and then traveling down and manifesting in our physical body.

While science and medicine search for cures, some awesome in their discoveries and some terribly corrupt and damaging, only God knows the truth of illness.

God is gracious; He allows us to walk in paths that are not of truth but deception. Why? Because only by experiencing darkness can we come into the revelation of light and truth. We must choose the light, lest we remain in the darkness.

So come along and share my journey, and know this: I only see in part. I do not have the whole story, just my piece of the puzzle so far. I, too, am a work in progress, ever seeking more and more knowledge, greater revelation, and insight.

Who Am I?

When people meet me today and experience the power God has put in me, they automatically think I was raised in the church. This is so far from the truth.

I was raised in southwestern Pennsylvania, in the South Hills, outside of Pittsburgh. I lived in what was called the upper-middle class back then, and who knows how that calculates today.

My house was a three-story English Tudor, and I claimed the entire third floor as my domain. My father was one of two sons born to Swedish immigrants but wealthy ones; he was raised in Evanston, Illinois, a very upscale community.

My mother came from simple farmer roots, growing up in Ohio, where her ancestors settled when they immigrated from Scotland. She was raised in the Methodist church, where she got a lot of religion, but never met the man named Jesus.

My father's parents left Sweden partially due to the mandates of the Lutheran church, so he was raised with a rejection of all religious things. My grandfather immigrated to America in 1920 and made a fortune in Chicago; he was a genius in math and physics. The Swedish men prided themselves on their high intellect and disdained anything they could not see or that defied their logic.

The only time I went to church was Easter when we visited my grandmother in Ohio. I was water baptized in the little Methodist church in Savannah, Ohio.

An interesting note here, which will play a large part later in this book, is that my mother's parents got divorced when she was nine.

My grandfather remarried. He was a Mason from a long line of Masons, going back to the Scottish roots, and my step-grandmother was a Daughter of the Eastern Star. Here is a long line of the antichrist spirit, which has played a huge role in both world history and American history.

In my younger years, I felt a strong rejection of the church; I did not like going and made my objections known. There was a short season of church going when I was in elementary school. My parents took us to the Methodist church and made me go to Sunday school. I think my mother felt some niggling of guilt and tried to get some religion in our upbringing. I always felt so out of place and different from the other kids. They all knew the Bible stories and their scriptures, and I just felt stupid. I hated going, and the spirit of rebellion rose in me. I remember my parents then took me with them to the adult church service. I refused to participate in worship and sat and read a book. That attempt at fostering religion in me without the presence of the Holy Spirit did not still well with my little untrained spirit. My mother was trying to place on my sister and me the very thing she later rejected...the religious spirit.

When my mother married my father, she, too, became an unbeliever, conforming to his rejection of God and religion.

My father was an alcoholic who traveled for his job as a salesman. He was gone all week, and when he was home, he drank and demanded perfection and had no tolerance for small children. We got the belt for any small infraction of the rules, and I learned to live in fear and with a spirit of rejection.

I have only one sister, who is fifteen months older. She was always vying for attention and was always asking if they loved her. I think I got shoved to the back burner in the face of her great need to be noticed.

I believe my sister was jealous that I was born. Later on God showed me this is the same spirit that influenced Cain and Abel, a spirit of envy and jealousy. My mother was overwhelmed with having two daughters back-to-back and discovering she was married to an angry alcoholic. She never protected us from him; I believe she was afraid of him and had a fear of losing him and being rejected (like her father rejected her) if she stood up to him. My memories of my mother are of her always reading a book and ignoring what went on in a life she could not control.

We lived a good life, financially. We traveled to Europe and went on ski vacations and down to Cancun. Every summer, we went to Palm Beach to stay with my grandparents.

There was never any lack, and my sister and I went to one of the best school systems in the nation back then.

It is interesting how we, as children, adapted to a dysfunctional family unit. My sister became a perfectionist, straight A's, honor roll, captain of the cheerleaders, anorexic and bulimic.

I adopted the spirit of rebellion. I cut school, drank, smoked, did drugs, was promiscuous, and was thrown out of high school a month before graduation—two radical reactions to the same situation. The perfectionist craves love and says, "look at me," thinking, *If I do everything perfectly, you will love me.* The rebellious one says, "no matter what I do, it's not good enough, so the hell with everything."

I spent years traveling, drinking, partying, and trying to discover who I was...I never did.

When you are devoid of a life with spiritual influence, a life where you do not personally know your Creator, all you have is what society and your parents tell you who you should be. I was taught I needed a successful career, a house in the suburbs, nice furnishings, a husband, two children, and a dog. My restless spirit could not wrap my mind around this conformity. Who was I really? I was such a rebel, and my father was always telling me I would never amount to anything without this great education that I rejected. So I felt doomed.

The negative words spoken over me and to me allowed the spirit of rejection to enter my life when I was very young. Spirits need a doorway to enter, and it comes in many forms like words spoken, physical abuse, verbal abuse, traumatic experiences, and so on. We are not aware as children, so we learn to cope with all that the best we can. We develop coping mechanisms to the pain, whether it be OCD, stomach problems, night terrors, eating disorders, or a whole list of other issues, just trying to shut off and bury this negative poison.

God Has a Plan

Even when you do not know God, He is orchestrating a plan for your redemption and destiny. This is so evident to me now as I look back to my very first job.

At seventeen, I got a job at the local Health Food store, Back to Nature. I worked with a wonderful woman there, Edith, who helped me understand and regulate my blood sugar problems. Hypoglycemia ran in my mother's side of the family. It was an eye-opener in helping sustain energy, focus, and mood stability. It was also my introduction to the effects of diet and supplements and their impact on health in a very basic way. This woman was also the one who introduced me to the art of using a pendulum in discerning positive and negative energies. Her husband was a gemologist, and he made me my very own pendulum, out of a very specific stone, that "vibed" with my energy. It was an introduction to the occult that, in my innocence, I found very cool and spiritual.

It was in this little shop that I discovered a small book on the rack that identified wild medicinal plants. Funny how that book called my name, grabbed my attention, and never let it go. God has a destiny that will not be denied, even when you do not know Him. I was seventeen when I began my foray and study into herbalism.

I remember vividly being at a High School graduation party, out in the country, at an old log cabin. I had my wildcrafting book with me, and as I sat on the front porch, I was staring intently at a mass of tall plants growing across the road in the cow pasture. I was sure it was boneset. I dared to ease my way through the barbed wire and gather an armful.

What a find! Boneset was one of the first plants introduced to the Jamestown settlement by the Indians. It was called "boneset" due to its ability to cure the influenza that felt like your bones were breaking. It is also so rich in minerals that it helps set broken bones. Shortly after that, I moved out to Boulder, Colorado, and I packed my suitcase with dried boneset. It came in handy, and I helped many overcome the initial signs of illness. This plant will nip a cold or flu in the bud if used at the onset of symptoms.

While in Boulder for those few years, it was very hip to have your astrology chart read, and I had mine read and professionally charted. There was much reading of astrology, tarot cards, discussion of out-of-body travel, and all things New Age. In the years prior, during high school, I would go down to visit my friend at college at West Virginia University. It was there I met a man named Phil, right out of the '60's free love movement, who introduced me to the *Seth Material* books.

Seth was an entity channeled by Jane Roberts. It was all about alternate realities and was a highly intellectual read. Intellectualism is one of the ways the devil tries to deceive. It all sounds so spiritual, so very difficult to understand that you think you are evolving on the spiritual plane, but in reality, intellectualism takes you further from God. Jesus made the good news simple to understand so that even a child could grasp its concept.

During my 20s, I became more engrossed in spiritualism and dabbled in astrology, numerology, and the New Age readings of the likes of Shirley McClain. Boy, I thought I was really smart and advancing in the spiritual realm. I continued to use my pendulum to "divine" energies.

Wake Up Call

In 1989 I married a man; I probably should not have. I say this because we came from two very different backgrounds and education histories: I was an upper-middle-class snob, and he was a simple country boy. I had two children with him, for which I am forever grateful and blessed.

We lived the high life; he built me a wonderful home, bought me anything I wanted, and boy, did I know how to spend! We both drank heavily, and the party was on all the time. But there is always a price to pay, and mine was a controlling husband. He started alienating me from my friends and family. He would drink and act terribly in their presence so that I would make excuses not to see my parents or friends. His friends were just fine, and his dead parents were on the platform of angels. He got a lot of Sunday school and religion in his youth but never met the man named Jesus.

My son was three and my daughter five when I had the great meltdown. I remember standing at the sink, snapping beans for dinner and crying, thinking, *Is this all there is?* I felt empty and frustrated; I recall the thought that there was something out there that I was missing; I just did not know what it was. Without anyone to counsel me, and I mean spiritually and emotionally, I began to rebel. I was repeating the pattern of my childhood because that was all I knew. I did know it was wrong, but I did not have anyone to point out a better way.

So many of you out there are doing the same thing, repeating dysfunctional patterns because you cannot see any other way. When you do not have the Holy Spirit living in you to be the teacher and the way maker, you follow spiritual entities that have attached and influenced your family line for generations.

Much the same way you inherit fifty percent of your DNA from both parents, you also inherit the spiritual forces that come down the family line. For example, the spirit of addiction that came down from both my father's and mother's side was manifesting itself clearly in my life back then. I was addicted to alcohol, cigarettes, and drugs. Then, the spirit of adultery raised its ugly head.

I thought my answer to my unhappiness in my marriage was another man who would worship me the way I needed. I was looking for love because I never received love from my parents. What we search for is the Heavenly Father's love, but not knowing this, we search for it in the flesh.

When I told my husband that I wanted a divorce (I was his third wife who wanted yet another divorce), he went ballistic and turned extremely revengeful. I worked for his company, so he retaliated (spirit of Bitterness) and cut off my finances. I had no money for a lawyer, and he hired the most expensive one money could buy. He was violent, and one time tried to choke me. He destroyed fine antiques so I would not want to take them. This is called the spirit of Bitterness; it operates with seven spirits: Unforgiveness, Retaliation, Revenge, Hatred, Wrath, Violence, and Murder, including murder with the tongue (your words). It is a fine example of a generational spirit that comes down the line.

The day he took my car away was the breaking point. I felt like a rat in a cage, being poked and prodded with no way out. I was in torture. Yes, Jesus's words are true—the devil comes to steal, kill, and destroy.

When he took my car and left for work, I locked him out of the house. We never locked our house, and neither of us carried keys to the house. When he came home and could not get in the garage, he went to the back deck and pounded at the door. My little three-year-old son ran from behind me and unlocked the door! My husband came in, and I was in such a rage (spirit of Bitterness) that I took the kitchen chairs (heavy wooden

Windsor) and, with supernatural strength, started flinging the chairs at him! Fury is fueled by the spiritual powers of darkness. During this tornado of rage, I looked over and saw my small children hiding in fear behind the couch. This broke the spell and woke me up. I ran upstairs in mortal horror at what I had become and locked myself in the guest room, where I had moved months before.

I remember being on my knees, sobbing and saying, "God, if You are real, I need You, and I need You now!" Not really expecting a response, I crawled into bed and fell asleep.

The next thing I knew, I was kneeling before the Throne of the Lord. The angels were all around, and they were singing, "Holy, Holy, Holy, Lord God Almighty, who was, and is and is to come." Then I saw myself as if I was floating in space, and there were arrows of light that were being shot into my body. I became filled with this light, and I knew I was being "Born in The Spirit." I do not know how I knew this terminology, as I was not churched and had not read the Bible...except for the Spirit of the Living God was speaking into me.

I awoke with a whole new understanding of life with a side of me that was unknown and now had been birthed. I knew there was God, that He knew me and heard me! I was filled with a new life and purpose.

The Lord continued to give me dreams and encounters in the night. Even in my limited understanding of His nature, I knew He was teaching and imparting His Spirit into me.

One encounter stands out to me vividly, just like it happened yesterday. I had a particular "dream" that lasted for thirty days. Every night, I was taught the art of the laying of the hands to heal the sick. I did not have the understanding as to who was teaching me; I only knew it was feminine, mighty, and holy. I came to learn years later that it was a Healing Angel. It was very literally a school. I felt as if I was not really asleep but living in a parallel reality. The Angel would teach, and I would sometimes wake up and say, "Yes, I understand," and then go back into the encounter. At the end of the thirty days, the Angel said, "Now it is your turn," meaning the authority and gift were now given to me. The last thing this Angel said to me that I will *never* forget is, "Remember, it is not you, but the Love of God that works through you."

There was so much other knowledge imparted during that time that I have not tapped into or used, and I believe it will come to pass at its appointed time. For instance, I was shown how certain notes like middle C, when held for a prolonged time, have a corresponding color and vibration that, when released, change the pattern of the cells to bring healing. Much has been done in this area but has been suppressed by the demonic powers of greed in the medical field. Healing all comes from God; it is His very nature. It is our abandonment of His divine plan that brings spiritual sickness and physical disease.

It was shortly after this experience that I was contemplating what to do to make money. I told God I never want to go back to a nine-to-five job ever again.

While at the gym later in the week, my aerobics instructor, Rose, said, "Wendy, I saw this ad in a horse magazine for equine massage; I think you would love this." God uses people to lead and guide you onto His path for your life. I called the number in the ad and found out it was $750.00 for the course! I was devastated; all my finances were cut off.

The next day in the mail, a check arrived for $950.00 from our escrow account—I drove straight to the bank, cashed the check, and enrolled in the course.

The Devil Tries to Take Me Out

The next week, I drove from Pittsburg to Round Hill, Virginia, for the Equissage training. I was leaving a few days earlier to stop and visit my friend Debbie and her husband, who lived outside of DC.

While driving the Pennsylvania Turnpike, on a clear sunny winter day, I encountered the enemy.

Cruising at seventy or eighty miles per hour in the outside lane, a semi-truck came barreling along, passing me in the inside lane. Halfway past me, it started moving over into my lane!

I was driving a big Lincoln Town car, and I had a concrete barrier on my left dividing the highway. I remember thinking, *Okay, God, this is how I'm going to die.* I saw myself hitting the barrier and flipping over into the oncoming traffic, and being completely obliterated by it.

The semi's wheels crushed in my passenger side. I know now that it was my surrendering to God that saved me. I do not know who was driving my car—I have no recollection of having my hands on the wheel. The peace of God consumed the atmosphere in my vehicle.

I was driving at seventy miles an hour in that small space with the concrete barrier on my left and the semi's wheels shearing off my passenger side. I remember when the outside mirror flipped inward and shattered the window. Beautiful prisms of light, all colors of the rainbow were floating peacefully through the air. There was absolute perfect peace inside my car as the hand of God saved my life.

The semi passed, and we both pulled over to the side of the Turnpike. My entire passenger side was crushed in, and the window shattered, but my car was drivable. The driver of the truck was horrified at what he had done and kept saying, "I never saw you."

Of course, he did not; the enemy intended to take me out before I could fulfill my spiritual destiny. But what the enemy intends for evil, God turns for good. I now knew the saving hand of God. Years later, I had a revelation that our lives are not our own. If your time is up, it is up. He has the power to keep you here or take you home to Him. You have no control over the decision. So, surrender.

The paramedics came along with highway safety. Those paramedics were astounded that my heart rate and blood pressure were completely normal! I experienced no adrenaline rush. The peace of God was still with me. They boarded up my window, and I was back on my way.

This incident happened just shortly after I was born into the Kingdom of God. The enemy was trying hard to take me out: he knows the plans God has for us, and for him, it always means the end of his power over us.

I arrived at my friend's house on Friday afternoon and was planning to spend the weekend before going to Equissage on Monday.

All hell broke loose that night as the worst snowstorm in a twenty-year history hit DC and Virginia! We received three feet of snow, and the two states who were ill-prepared for blizzards came to a screeching halt. I was snowed in for a week.

It was yet another divine plan by my Father in Heaven. He watches over us and prepares a table before us in the presence of our enemies.

You see, all those who were flying in for the weeklong training at Equissage had to cancel. Only I and another girl drove in. When the roads got plowed, the owners of Equissage met me in the nearest town and drove me in because you had to have four-wheel drive. The other woman and I stayed in Mary's basement because all the hotels were closed. She fed us and gave us private training.

What I had not counted on when I left was that I would need hotel and food money. I was in such a season of stress that I just took the money and ran.

But God! He provided food and shelter by way of a storm. There is perfect peace in the middle of the storm!

When I took my final test, which was a total body massage on one of Mary's horses, I experienced my first miracle. When I finished the massage, I tied the horse's lead rope in the corner of the stall and went out to tell Mary I was finished.

When Mary entered, she stood there looking astounded. I could not figure out why she was so flabbergasted. The horse was peacefully tied in the corner, almost asleep, totally relaxed. When Mary recovered, she said that this horse had never been able to be tied due to a traumatic experience in his past. If you tried to tie him to a spot, he would go ballistic; yet here he was, in total peace. Only God could do these things. I was just beginning to see the miracles God would perform on these magnificent creatures.

I did not know it then, but I know now that Jesus Himself rides a white horse! I am writing these words twenty-two years later, and I can testify that I have ridden with Jesus on that white horse.

The Miracles Begin

After my divorce, I moved onto a horse farm where I had been working. I was partnering with the caretaker of the farm, Bill, a man who was old schooled in training and driving racehorses. We operated a rehabilitation and recovery business for them, being just five miles from the Meadows racetrack in Washington, Pennsylvania.

A few months before moving to the farm, I flew down to Palm Beach Gardens to stay with my mom. My parents had inherited my great aunt's condo and would move there permanently a few years later. I was at a terrible crossroads in my life, not knowing which direction to go. I recall standing on the beach and crying out to God. I had this sudden inspiration (the Holy Spirit at work!) that I wanted to go to school. Not just any school, but to be trained in natural health.

When I returned to Washington, I happened to meet a woman who offered to do some brochures for our farm. It was this total stranger who said, "I think you should go to this school." That school happened to be Trinity School of Natural Health. I began my studies in the fall of 1997 in Naturopathy and later in Master Herbalism. It was the beginning of my introduction to using all that God has created for our health.

My passion for herbs and wildcrafting plants was reborn in that season. God is so incredibly amazing, and He placed me on a hundred-acre farm, resplendent with many different herbs for my experimental pleasure!

I began to look at food differently, too. I understood there had to be purity and life-giving properties to the foods we ate. Growing up, we did not have junk food, but it was the beginning of industrialized packaged food that has destroyed the health in America. I remember when Chef Boyardee's lasagna came out in a box. My sister and I would have that if my parents went out to dinner: my mother grew up on a farm in Ohio and always prepared homegrown food. When one of the first McDonalds opened, she got sick after eating one of their hamburgers and would never eat there again. Her body naturally rejected their processed junk. How blind and insensitive we have become to the signals of distress our bodies send out!

The Lord was also revealing to me the poisoning of the mind. I would sit out in this vast empty pasture by the running creek and talk to God for hours. I would be practicing breathing in His pure cleansing breath and expel all my worry, anxiety, fear, and a whole host of bad feelings. Much later, this simple exercise would begin to play a huge role in my healing and help others release the sin of this world that so contaminates us.

It amazes me to this day what a wonderful training ground God placed me in during this initial season in my early spiritual awakening. I had the privilege of practicing my healing gift of the laying on of hands and using herbs and food to rehabilitate an entire barn of racehorses. Racehorses are some of the most abused animals on this planet. The way they are overworked, drugged, and treated for greed, money, and power is a terrible crime.

Since Bill was old schooled, he did not believe in my fancy-dancy equine massage training. I offered my services for free to an old racehorse belonging to the owner of the farm.

Monkey, as she was known, was getting on in her career and a bit tired and sore. I worked on her poor tight muscles for a week before her next race.

The night she raced, she flew along the track to win! A refreshed and revived old girl.

The owner said to me, "I don't know what you did, but keep doing it!" It was a joy to my spirit to see the gift of healing!

One day, Bill came home from the track with a beautiful gelding named Mix Me One. His only problem was that he was three-legged and dead lame. I found out he had broken the coffin bone in his right front and fractured his pastern, and this was a year ago—they had just thrown him out in the pasture for a year and expected him to heal.

When they brought him back to the track to train, the poor boy just laid down and would not get up. They were going to sell him for dog meat when Bill stepped in and offered to buy him.

Bill was always looking to make it big in an industry he had grown up in but had never achieved any success. He knew Mix was a high-dollar winner and had confidence the horse could be rehabilitated. Little did I know he was looking to me to do the work. Bill saw in me a talent I did not know I possessed.

I spoke to the vets (there were five!) that had treated him when he was injured. All five said the same thing, "That horse will never race again."

I remember walking down to the barn after talking with the vets. I looked up to the heavens and asked God, "So what do I do now?"

I very clearly heard God say, "Will you listen to what man says, or will you listen to me?" When God presents you with a choice, always choose His way, however impossible.

He started speaking to me in pictures and words in my mind. I was to get some comfrey root and pick some boneset and lobelia down at the creek. I used these to make a strong tea, and, twice-daily, I soaked a wrap in the tea and wrapped Mix's leg around the ankle and up the pastern. Boneset is high in minerals and will set bones as will comfrey root. I put the foot in a boot with a pad saturated in the herbal medicine.

I then knelt at his leg, placed my hands, and prayed for God's divine healing, twice daily. I also ordered an herbal tincture, a high mineral complex, that contained alfalfa, dandelion, kelp, yellow dock, and nettles, and fed him a tablespoon two times daily. I was learning through my Naturopathic studies that the body needs high doses of alkaline minerals to repair.

We are literally made of the dust of the Earth, and that dust is of pure minerals. However, man and animal use the organic living minerals that plants create out of the inorganic dust.

That is why God says, "every seed-bearing plant on the face of the whole earth...will be yours for food" (Genesis 1:29 NIV).

One quirk about Mix was that he would not step up into the bath stall. Obviously, he had some bad memories of the things done to him. The bath stall was enclosed on three sides and open in the front to step up onto the mats. There, the Lord taught me a lesson on will. Since I could not force Mix up into the stall, I had to make him want to come.

I stepped up into the stall, turned around, and faced him, and knelt down. He was on a long lead line, standing outside the stall. I did not look at him but bowed my head. He was standing there with his head flung back, pulling on the rope. I just knelt there. After a few minutes, I sensed in the spirit that he was bowing his will down to mine. I was picturing him in my mind, stepping up into the stall. He started softening, then dropped his head, and finally stepped up into the stall! Victory, and it was his decision. Healing is always dropping your will to receive His will for you. That is why God says, "submit to me."

As the weeks passed, I continued my ministrations with prayer, herbs, and a sound diet. I would lead Mix out to pasture every day, and he went from hobbling out to walking sounder and more confidently every day.

Oh, what a thrill to my spirit was the day I led him out, and he took off on a trot and kicked up his heels! Hard work and prayer pay off—never give up! The impossible is only around the corner.

Now here goes the most interesting part of the story. We raced this horse, and he raced well. Bill did not stress Mix by racing him in his former class of horses but in a lower one. He raced well and would be sore on that foot after, but with continued therapy and prayer, he would show no sign of pain. We decided to have him X-rayed. The X-ray showed the foot and pastern were still broken! Now how is it possible to race and walk soundly with a broken leg? All I can say is that only God can take away all pain.

I saw this many years later in an associate pastor at my church. He was bent over and had a huge hump in his spine from scoliosis. My sister has scoliosis, and it is very painful. This man had no pain because God healed him at a Katheryn Kullman meeting in Pittsburgh. He never experienced any pain after that touch from God, yet visibly, he had a very crooked spine. We will never understand the mystery of God.

Not long after the healing of Mix, Bill brought home a horse from the track that had blown out her suspensory ligament. She was hobbling on three legs and could not bear weight on her left front foot. Bill came into the kitchen, told me there was a mare down at the barn, and to go "fix her." Like I said, he had a belief about me that I did not see yet.

I took her out of the stall and placed her in cross ties. She would not bear weight on the foot, and the ligament was clearly blown out with a large swelling. I remember I just stood there looking at that leg and pondering in my mind what to do. I heard the whisper of God saying, "pray." I knelt down and placed my hands around that leg, and all I kept saying was, "I believe." I recalled the angel who taught me the laying on of the hands in the night season. I held that picture in my mind of the perfect love of God coming into the tissues and restoring the cells. I must have knelt there for full five minutes, just repeating out loud, "I believe."

Suddenly boom! There was an electric current that ran through me and into the mare. I fell backward of the force of it. The mare first startled with the feel of it, then settled. I looked, and holy moly, she was standing sound, and there was no swelling—completely healed in a moment!

I was wide-eyed with wonder; I unhooked her from the cross ties, and she walked soundly back into her stall with a look of total peace upon her. I walked back to the house, into the kitchen, and said to Bill, "Okay, she has been healed." He just looked at me, not knowing what to believe.

But the next morning, he looked at her leg, saw it looked normal, and put her out to pasture. She took off at full gallop, no injury in sight!

What an awesome God!

Walk Into Deception

The entire time these miracles were happening, I was not in a church; I was simply following God the best I knew how. What I knew was that He was a God that teaches, and He heard me and answered me. So, I would sit for hours in the field, talking to Him and listening for His voice. Little did I know how incredibly valuable that training was.

One night, I had a very powerful dream. I dreamt of a high field, where the tops of the trees were only visible. The cows were grazing on the left and the horses on the right. The grass was lush and tall with growth.

God was in the sky! The color was so blue, so vibrant, and so alive I just knew (in the dream) it was Him who watches over me. Also, in the sky, out of the right side came a line of sheep; "My sheep listen to my voice...they follow me" (John 10:27 NIV). The sheep were surreal and were all lining up and forming a perfect circle in the sky. The circle was incomplete as the sheep continued to come into the line.

I was driving a wagonload of people across the field to the gate with a team of horses. Following close at the back of the wagon was a two-story sow. Yes, a huge, gigantic pig! It represented the devil, and its foul breath was filled with evil intent. Interestingly, I had no fear in the dream but the perfect peace of God. As I drove the people, the sow was hot on our heels. I drove through the gate, and when the sow tried to follow through the gate, it shrunk into a little itty-bitty pig and went screaming all the way home. "But the gate is narrow, and the way is straitened and compressed, that leads away to life, and few are those who find it" (Mathew 7:14 AMP).

I told Bill about this dream. At the time, I did not have the spiritual capacity to understand it. It was not until 2013, when God called us to South Carolina, that I finally understood the meaning. The year of the dream was 1998. Fifteen years passed between the prophetic dream, and now, in 2020, it is coming to pass.

Bill listened and said, "Your dream is in this book my cousin has; we will go over to Ohio and talk to him." Wow, I was excited—my dream was foretold in some book! How awesome was that?

We drove a couple of hours over to Ohio, and his cousin, who was somewhat of a hermit, listened to my dream and handed me a huge thick book. He said he had not read the whole of it, but it was possible my dream was in there. He believed in this book and the revelation it contained. In fact, this book is referred to as the *Fifth Epochal Revelation* to our planet.

Well, let me tell you this book was a huge intellectual journey, filled with The Word (Scripture) and revelation of events such as the "Lucifer Rebellion" and "the Life and Teaching of Jesus Christ." I was enamored with the insight and told my friend Jane about the book. Jane searched and found a study group, and we both agreed we would attend.

We went to the home of a very prominent member of social standing on the North Side of Pittsburgh. There were a fairly large group of women present, and we sat around her dining room table and discussed the book. Then, I remember Beebe saying, "Now the spirits are going to speak, you may get thirsty for water, so please fill your glass."

In the past, I had read Shirley McClain and Jane Roberts, so I was excited as a woman named Gerdean began to allow these spirits to speak through her. It was a very intellectual reading, filled with words of encouragement and love for those of us still struggling on this planet. I was told that these spirits were people that had once lived on this planet, and their job now was to help us navigate the way of life here and understand how the Lucifer rebellion had introduced sin into the planet. They were also to guide us further into our relationship with Jesus, whom they called by another name. Sounds so wonderful, right?

The enemy is very intelligent and crafty. He has been at this for thousands of years, and he weaves truth amidst deception.

This group of women became my very good friends, and I would travel an hour every Thursday up to the North Side to listen and learn. I discovered that there were groups of believers all over the US and even across the world that followed this book. I thought I was so smart and superior because I was reading it and listening to dead spirits giving their wisdom. Almost everyone in these groups had been burned in some form or another by religion. None of them went to church but had grabbed ahold of this higher knowledge.

I became good friends with Gerdean, one of the transmitters of spiritual entities, and would often stay at her house in Butler instead of driving back to the farm. Gerdean thought I was prostituting myself by staying on the farm with Bill. He had come to a few meetings but could not stand all the feminine energy. He was in love with me, but I did not return the affection; he was a good and dear friend, nothing more.

I began to distance myself from the farm and Bill and spend more and more time with Gerdean and the spiritual group. They eventually trained me as a transmitter of these disembodied spirits.

When you open yourself up to this realm, they will happily come and take residence. You think you are highly "spiritual," but you are actually entertaining the fallen angels. But even when you choose the path of darkness, God is there, allowing you to make your choices but ever steering you towards the light.

The First Divine Move

One day, when I was online following the group discussion, I came across a notice for an event called Spiritual Nights. It was to be held in Florida on the beach.

Oh, how I wanted to go, yet it seemed impossible. I did not have the money, nor did I know anyone in this group in Florida. I remember sitting there yeaning to go, and I heard that still small voice say, "You will go." I dismissed this because of the impossibility. But God had a plan!

Not long after that, I went over to a horse farm to massage a horse for a first-time client. That poor horse had been locked in his stall for six months due to a conformation deformity in his back pasterns. In that season of equine massage, God opened up a realm of communication between me and the horses I was working on. If I tuned in, I could hear their thoughts in my mind. Not in words, but a wave of emotion would translate into what they were feeling. This poor horse was so depressed. He would never heal in body or emotion until he was allowed to run free as he was created to do. The owners had said that if he could not be fixed, they would put him down.

Now, I do not recommend anyone doing what I did, but I made a decision that I was going to let him run free...and I did. Wow, was he happy! He took off across the pasture and kicked up his heels. I knew his last hurrah was a joyous one. Naturally, the owners were furious, and I probably ruined my career and reputation, but I felt rebellious and reckless.

Rebellion is what Lucifer did. He thought himself superior to God, so the spirit of rebellion that drove me as a child, teenager, and young adult was still controlling my actions. I did not see this or understand the spirit behind it because I thought myself superior in thought to those around me. This is the spirit of pride that came down in my generation from my father and grandfather's line.

This spirit continued to wreak havoc back at my farm. I got into a huge fight with Bill, mostly because I did not return his feelings towards me. I felt like I was in another trap, and I fought my way out by burning bridges.

I ran upstairs to call Gerdean and maybe find some sane advice, and she informed me that she and a few others had decided they were going to drive to Florida for Spiritual Weekend. Talk about divine providence! I told her I was coming and would pack a bag and drive up to Butler that night.

I never told Bill I was leaving for four days. I assumed he would feed my dog Sam, who stayed outside. Sam was my buddy, and I got him as a little puppy in a hardware store in West Virginia. Bill would never allow him in the farmhouse, but he was by my side all day long as I worked with the horses. I said goodbye to Sam and drove off. Little did I know this was the catalyst for a whole new chapter in my life.

We arrived in Cape San Blas, an incredibly beautiful beach in the Panhandle. A member of the Florida group owned a beach house there, so that was the central location for gathering. Beach houses had been rented to accommodate everyone. There were people from all over the country. They represented the different groups in various states, such as Idaho, Virginia, California, Massachusetts, etc. I was thrilled to be a part of this spiritual family.

I immediately took a long walk on the beach. It was February and a bit chilly, but the sun was out, and I was free! Oh, how I love the beach, to splash in the surf and feel the glorious sun. I came back to the main house refreshed and ready for adventure.

I remember sitting on the sofa, getting acquainted with the rest of the early arrivals, when a gorgeous man came in the back door of the kitchen. I noticed him immediately.

It was not so much his looks, and he was good-looking, but it was his spirit that called to mine. It was like a glow was around him.

Leigh immediately introduced us, and from that moment on, we were inseparable for the next four days.

Yes, we fell in love quickly, and we knew we were meant to be together. Like I said before, it was not an attraction of lust but the spirit. We just knew we had a destiny together.

Interestingly, after a horrible divorce and then moving in with Bill, I had told God that I would not be with another man unless He picked him for me. I confessed to Him that I did not know how to choose men wisely and asked Him if he would do the choosing for me. I was prepared to wait for years for the right one to come along.

When I returned to the farm after Florida, I immediately began to pack up my belongings, and there was a lot! I had had a stirring in my spirit for many months before this that I would not be here much longer, so I had begun the process of preparing to move.

The first thing I noticed when I got back to the farm was that my dog was gone. I panicked and was calling

Bill on his cell, and he was not answering! I kept asking God, "Where is Sam? Where is Sam?" I kept hearing Him say, "I have taken care of him." I did not know what that meant, and I thought maybe He took my dog to heaven.

Bill finally called me back, and all he would say is that Joyce had my dog. You see, we lived in a stone cottage-style farmhouse, and the owners of the farm lived high above us on the hill. John and Joyce lived in the main house. I trucked up that hill so fast; it was like my feet had wings—I was in great shape with all the farm work.

In talking with Joyce, I got the full picture of what went on while I was gone. Poor Sam had waited at the bottom of the drive for me to come home. There was a pack of wild dogs in the area that had gone after our goat once. It seems that Sam took up with these dogs (or so Bill told me later). The stray dogs were going after the chickens and the goat again, and Sam was in with the whole crew.

Joyce happened to drive up the farm driveway and saw Bill aiming to shoot Sam! She quickly got Sam into her car and took him home with her. Now, in the two years I had been living there, Joyce had come to the farm once! What are the odds that she came at the moment Bill intended to kill my dog?

But God! It is just proof that He is always watching over us. Not only did Joyce recuse Sam, but she and

John fell in love with him and wanted to keep him. I was so thankful because I knew that I had to move up to Butler to stay with Gerdean, and I could not bring Sam. God truly arranges everything for us in advance.

It was with dragging feet and a heavy heart that I packed my belongings and moved out of this beautiful hundred-acre farm. I am a nature lover, and the thought of moving to Butler, a depressed steel town, and living on Main street above Gerdean's book store made me sad. I knew I had to go, and I asked God how long I would be there. His answer was, "three months." That I could live with, and I did live it well.

I got a job with the top horse barn during the worst winter on record. I had to park overnight on Main St, and every morning the snowplow would bury my car, and every morning I had to shovel it out at 6 a.m. I truly loved cleaning stalls and taking care of the horses. There were thirty stalls I had to clean on a daily basis. Good thing God told me to get in shape.

During this time, Dennis and I were emailing back and forth, making plans. He paid to have my own phone installed upstairs so we could have private conversations. This was 1999, and we did not own cell phones yet; it was the time of dial-up internet and good old-fashioned phones. Dennis flew up several times, and I flew to Tallahassee, Florida, where he lived.

Dennis decided he would trade in his parents' motorhome and purchase a newer one. We had a plan to first travel with all our children and then travel the West together in the motorhome. He and his children, Josh 10 and Missy 8, picked me up with my children, Ginger 8 and David 7, at my parents' house in Pittsburgh. We traveled to the Finger Lakes in New York and stayed with a friend of his, and then went on to Toronto to visit his older sister Pam and her husband. We had a wonderful time, and the kids got along fine.

I say fine, but in reality, children have their own demons from divorce. When trauma, whether physical or emotional, comes into a child's life, they have to learn to cope with it in any way they can. The experience opens a door for negative spirits to enter. They may feel like one parent, or both do not love them, so enters a spirit of rejection. They may hate the parent who chooses to leave the house and the marriage. This opens a door for the spirit of bitterness and the seven spirits that come under this stronghold: unforgiveness, retaliation, revenge, anger, wrath, violence, and murder (including murder with the tongue or your words). These are called doorways in the spiritual realm and will and can affect your entire life if you let them. Both of our children acted out occasionally, but by and large, it was a good experience.

After a month, we returned our children to our ex-spouses, packed up Dennis' house he was renting, and set off for Vancouver, British Columbia, in the motorhome, towing the Jeep. We were off on a spiritual journey. We fully believed to grow in the spirit and encounter spiritual entities who would enlighten us to our path in life. There was a big gathering of followers to this spiritual group we belonged to in Vancouver. People from all over the world were coming to share in the light.

We got to the New Mexico border, and the motorhome blew the muffler. We kept driving, trying to get to Linda's house in Santa Fe. We made it, but the floor of the motorhome was melted underneath. We parked the damaged vehicle in her driveway (thank goodness for lots of space), packed all our belongings into the Jeep, and set off for the conference.

It was around this time that I began to experience my first bout of cystitis. I did not know what was wrong with me, only that I had to urinate frequently. We camped in various campgrounds along the way to Vancouver. We camped in Washington state, up by the Canadian border, and I was enthralled at the lushness of the forest and vegetation. I remember I had this thought continually in my mind to gather the giant horsetail (an herb) and make a tea to drink. This thought kept telling me it would heal my urinary problem. I did not do this because I was not yet filled with the Holy Spirit, and I did not realize this was the Lord speaking to me. This was His gift that He was trying to develop in me, but I did not trust this voice.

How very ironic that here I was, transmitting dead spirits, yet I did not trust or recognize the Spirit of the Living God! Satan is so good at what he does; he is the master deceiver. So, I suffered from this affliction for months before finally purchasing an herbal product in Utah that contained none other than horsetail!

So why the sudden affliction of the bladder? I now know it is the spirit of fear that works in the mind. I had a fear of the unknown, fear of leaving my children, fear of what my ex would do, fear of what my parents thought, and fear of rejection. Fear goes down through the limbic system or the emotional channel in the body and targets the weakest organs. In my case, it was the adrenal/kidney. At this stage, I did not know that I had adrenal exhaustion from my last five years of turmoil. When the adrenals get deficient, it also causes kidney deficiency. So my cystitis was a manifestation of this constant fear that was draining me. Interestingly, in Chinese medicine, the kidney is associated with healthy transition through the different stages of life.

We arrived in Vancouver, and what started out as a high adventure ended up being one of the worst adventures. First, Dennis and I got into an argument, and he was not speaking to me. I was far from home and felt rejected. The spirit of rejection was ingrained in my spirit from early childhood. When you do not receive the love and validation from your earthly father, you can carry this familiar generational spirit into every relationship. You will say and do things to cause this rejection to manifest. It is a spirit that plays a tape in your mind whispering, "nobody has ever loved you, therefore why try? They will just leave you."

Second, I had called my parents and learned that my ex-husband was going to court to claim I had deserted my children and to have my parental rights revoked. I was in huge turmoil. I did not know how I would get home, and I knew Dennis did not want to go back. I cried and cried and finally decided that I had to go back to fight for my children.

When Dennis saw my resolve, he agreed to go back with me.

We set off across the Canadian Rockies. We camped every evening, and I must say Canada has the most extraordinary scenery. You can pull off the highways to camp beside beautiful rushing water and lush forestry—no cheesy KOA camping up there, just the magnificent outdoors.

Somewhere before Banff National Park, I called my parents, only to learn that my ex-husband had already gone to court, declared me a deserter, and had gotten full custody. There was no reason to go back right away. I was devastated and missed my children terribly. The doubt that I was actually following what God wanted me to do weighed heavily upon my conscience.

Dennis and I traveled through the Canadian Rockies, down into Glacier National Park, and on to Idaho, where we stayed with friends. From there, it was on to Utah. We had gotten a book called *Hiking and Hot Springs*, and we hiked and camped at many spectacular hot springs in Utah, Colorado, and New Mexico. From July to November, we traveled, and then it was time to go back.

We ended up in Tallahassee because Dennis owned the house he grew up in. I have to admit I had a rough time for the next two years. I was depressed. I felt hopeless. I could not understand why God stuck me in this ugly little house full of mold and so far from my children. I had no understanding that God was stripping me of many idols that would not serve His purposes.

Depression is a brutal condition of the mind, where hopelessness lives. It is said that it is not a spirit but a state where the spirit of a person has lost all energy to perform. The world looks bleak, and joy is a distant memory. I know this state, and I sank deep into it for the first two years after I left Pittsburgh with Dennis. The poor man did not understand, and it caused a great strain in our relationship. I was consumed with guilt

over leaving my children, and they missea .
I could find no joy in my new life because tha.
mean I could be happy without my children. I .
wracked with guilt and shame, which drove me deep
into depression.

John and Paula Sanford, in their book Healing the
Wounded Spirit, state that the most basic and common
cause of depression is a combination of performance
orientation and hidden unresolved emotional factors
of guilt, fear, resentment, and rejection.

Performance orientation can occur when a person,
such as myself, does not receive enough unconditional
love and acceptance from their parents. They then hold
the belief that if they measure up to the standards that
please their parents, they will be accepted. It is a never-
ending cycle of trying to please and measure up to a
standard that does not exist. I most certainly had the
guilt over leaving my children, the fear that I would lose
custody, the resentment towards Dennis for having us
end up so far away from them, and my ever-present
spirit of rejection. What a spiritual cocktail of demons.
Yet without discernment of the Holy Spirit, I did not
know they were real entities. And so, I suffered their
torment.

Then there was my disdain for this little house. I
had grown up in a gorgeous three-story English Tudor, and I was accustomed to the finer things in life.

The cracker box I was living in at that time was beneath my standards. This judgmental and critical spirit is a true destroyer of joy. It is true what the scripture says, "Judge not, that you be not judged" (Mathew 7:1 NKJV). When you judge something or someone, whatever you have judged will come upon you. I had grown up with this judgmental and critical spirit, and now what I had thought beneath me had come upon me. Spirits like this come down through the generations, eating away the insides of a person. They are like corrosive acid.

God uses all things for good, though, and He used this circumstance to show me that I was judging people by the house they lived in. And that I had the creative ability to change how this house looked. It took me years, but I transformed that house inside and out into a beautiful, inviting little house.

There was a two-year season, where I traveled every other month to Pittsburgh to see my children. When we settled in Tallahassee, I knew I had to find a lawyer to get my parental rights back. Everyone I talked to wanted a 10,000-dollar retainer, and I was broke. I finally called my friend Alice in New Mexico and asked her to talk to her father. I spent my entire teenage years in Alice's house and knew her father, a prominent Pittsburgh attorney, very well. She told me to visit him the next time I went to Pittsburgh.

God, in His infinite wisdom, is so fascinating. Right before I left for Pittsburgh, I had a dream about Alice's brother, Dan, who was killed by a drunk driver in his late 20s. In the dream, Dan was in heaven, and he had huge blue eyes. I knew it was Dan, yet he was very different; he radiated such wisdom and intelligence, so unlike his reckless personality on earth. He looked at me and said, "There is no cancer in heaven." At that point in my life, I was not actively praying for people, so all I knew was this was a message for his father, who ironically had had a cancerous tumor removed from his lung.

I met with Bob, Alice's father, in Pittsburgh. He was not a believer, and I looked him right in the eye and said, "I had a dream, and I saw Dan in heaven. He is alive and well, and he says there is no cancer in heaven." Bob had no idea what to do with that; he just sat there in shock and then quickly recovered and told me he would give my name to an attorney they used for family law. Hey, all you can do is deliver the message. Bob ended up dying from that cancer, and I am sure he remembered my words.

The attorney Bob gave my name to turned out to be a nice Jewish man. He agreed to take my case and told me to pay him monthly whatever I could. Now, this was God! All I could afford to pay him at that time was $50 a month. We had some discussions about God during the times I was in Pittsburgh for court hearings. How I wish now that I had known the Bible, the old testament, and the Word! Our conversations could have been so much richer. I was in Pittsburgh for a custody hearing on the day the terrorists flew into the Twin Towers. All hell broke loose in downtown Pittsburgh, and my attorney and I walked calmly to court, only to find it canceled. We had a discussion on being ready for catastrophic events as depicted in the end times.

My attorney got my parental rights fully restored. It took many court hearings and many trips to Pittsburgh, but I came out a winner. I have lost contact with him, and I can never, this side of heaven, thank him enough. It was two years later when a check I sent him returned. He had forgiven my debt! I figured out years later, after gaining knowledge of Jewish law, that every seven years, a Jew is to forgive their debtors. What an awesome God!

Go Into the
Church

Faithfully every week, my husband and I attended the spiritual group where we met. We met at the Unitarian Church and spent the evening being social and then transmitting spiritual entities. For the most part, this was just a social group. My husband got dissatisfied and left it, but I still hung on. We continued to have beach retreats every February, and it was always a wonderful time, meeting new friends. Dennis and I got married at the retreat in February of 2001, and we were blessed with our first child, Rachael, nine months later.

I had suffered depression off and on from 1999 to 2001. There was so much hopelessness and fear tormenting me night and day. I had my two best friends in our group, Stan and Lisa, praying for me. When Rachael was born, I prayed that I would be delivered out of this depression at the same time I delivered her. God answered my prayers, and the cloud of depression lifted at her birth. I would like to say it never came back, but in the later years, I learned to recognize the demonic thoughts and put a stop to their lies; I came out of agreement with them. If that failed, what never failed was calling my spirit warrior friends and telling them to pray for me and send the depression away. There is nothing like a solid Christian, filled with the Holy Spirit, to send demons on their way. Works every time!

It was the next year that a Pentecostal minister from Australia came to speak at our beach retreat. My good friends Stan and Lisa took to him immediately and started slowly divorcing themselves from the group and sat under Rob's biblical training and teaching of the Holy Spirit. Boy, did I despise this man! I was rude to him and walked out on his teaching of the Holy Spirit, and I rejected everything having to do with Christianity. I was angry, and I did not know why. I was dissatisfied with our spiritual group because there was nothing spiritual about them; it was just a social group no matter how many times the intentions were to "be more spiritually minded."

Now, the devil knows when his time is short, hence my anger at the One True God knocking at my door. It took a bit of rebellion on my part before I began to start questioning what I was doing in this group (nothing) and where was the Truth. I was intrigued by the accounts Stan and Lisa were giving of the fascinating things they were learning and the mission trips they were taking. It seemed like God did do miracles, and I had a craving for the God of miracles.

One day, I was sitting on my bed and talking to God. I had become depressed and despondent about our group. I wanted more, but I did not know what that more was. I recall I was having a conversation with God about sin. I asked him to remove every particle of sin from my body. There appeared to be some sort of discussion going on in the spiritual realm. Suddenly, I felt the atmosphere in the room shift. Out of the corner of my bedroom, I heard a voice say, "Go into the Church."

To say I was shocked is an understatement, but almost immediately, in the spirit of rebellion, I answered, "I don't do church." I sat there in silence. I began to realize that you do not tell God no. I did not think it was God the All-Magnificent, the Creator of all heaven and earth, but what went through my mind was an *Angel of the Lord*. So I said I was sorry. I was also wondering which church, because in the South, there is a church on almost every corner. I decided to ask, so I said, "Which Church?" He answered, "The way will be shown."

Well, now that was confusing. I wondered how He would show me the way, and I think I became a little obsessed. I was not exactly sure what "Go into the church" meant. Was I just to walk into a church? Two days later while sitting in my back yard, this same voice came out of the atmosphere and repeated "Go into the church." This time I answered " Which church?" and the answer was the same "The way will be shown."

I was scheduled to leave in a few days to visit my children in Pennsylvania. For the past year, my friend Dee had been letting me stay at her house in Ellwood City. My children and I had her nice big house to ourselves as Dee was seldom there. Dee had decided to move to Florida in 2002, and I had to struggle to find friends who would take us in. In a weird twist of events, my ex-sister-in-law, Donna (married to my ex-husband's brother), invited us to stay at her house. So, it was at this time I preparing to stay at their house.

The next thing I know, I get a call from my sister-in-law's sister, a woman I had met once years ago, who informed me (and was very rude about it, I might add) that Donna did not want me staying there anymore and hung up.

I was a bit frantic, to say the least, and got furious that Donna did not have the courage to call and tell me herself. I had court-ordered visitation, and I never missed it. I kept hashing it over with God, but he was not saying much. The only idea I got was to pack camping gear. Rachael was about eighteen months old, David around nine, and Ginger eleven. I could conceivably take them camping, and I had no other options. So, I packed the camping gear in the Previa van, and off Rachael and I went.

It was a trip filled with the divine plan of God. As I was cruising along the interstate, winding my way through the Virginia mountains, I suddenly heard a voice. Not an audible voice, but it was loud in my head. It said, "Slow down and get in the outside lane." So I slowed, coming around a mountain bend, and got into the outside lane. Oh, Holy Moly! I rounded that bend, and there was a woman lying in the inside lane. There had just been a car accident minutes before, and she had obviously been thrown out of the car.

Had God not intervened, I would have run over her as she was lying right in my path. I think by this time, I was shaking pretty good; it was all so surreal. I remember I asked God if I should stop and offer assistance. I heard immediately that this was not my ministry, that the angels were there and help was on its way. God knows best because had I stayed, the road would have been closed, and my narrow window of getting to pick up my kids at the appointed time would have been lost. My ex looked for every opportunity to make trouble with the court and label me an unfit mother.

I arrived on time, told my kids to go in and pack for camping, and off we went to Ohio Pyle, Pennsylvania. How nice everyone was at the campground! Women had their men get me firewood and start my fire. I am an old pro at camping so putting up the tent was a breeze. We had a really wonderful time hiking beside the rushing spring waters and roasting marshmallows.

When I put all the kids to bed, I sat around the campfire and talked to God. Now, this may sound weird, but I think God has you do weird things sometimes. Look at how many times in the Bible God asked people to do strange things in obedience, like in 2 Kings 5:10 (NLT): "But Elisha sent a messenger out to him with this message: 'Go and wash yourself seven times in the Jordan River. Then your skin will be restored, and you will be healed of your leprosy.'"

I heard the voice in my head tell me to walk down the road and stand in the dark shadows. I have to say, it was a bit scary as there was no moon that night, and the shadows were blacker than black. I went and stood in the shadows for a moment, and nothing happened. Just as I was thinking, there was a voice in my head leading me astray when I heard the Lord say, "Receive my Holy Spirit." I did not have flashes of light nor tongues of fire, but I felt as if a vortex was opening up in the heavens above my head. It seemed as if this light of living water was being poured into my mind. It was as if the dimensions had shifted, and now there was a new piece of the Father inside of me. I felt lighter, calmer, and more aware of His presence.

Sunday came, and it was time to pack up and leave the mountains, my kids had to go back to their father, and I had to find a place to stay for the week. All the way home from the mountains, I kept asking God where I could stay. I did not have money for a hotel. The only thing that kept coming to my mind was my old friend Valerie, who lived in Ellwood. I had not spoken to her in a few years as our lives changed, and I moved away. I stopped at a rest area and used the payphone to call her. I told her what was going on, and she welcomed me to stay at her place. She was living with some man, but I could make a bed in the living room. How God answers prayer! She was a lifesaver. Then, something really out of character happened.

Val was a lapsed, and I mean lapsed Catholic. Religion never ever came out of her mouth. Yet no sooner had I got there that she began to tell me of a little Baptist church she found right there in Ellwood. She was telling me how she felt compelled to go, and every time she went, she just wept. I knew I had to visit this church because I knew this was a divine appointment. God was using Valerie to show me this church. It just happened (no coincidence) that the church had renewal (kind of like revival) services the following Friday and Saturday. I planned to go and bring my kids.

The renewal was a Holy Ghost spirit-filled praise, worship, and altar call service. I had never experienced anything like it. You could feel the presence of God in that place. I recall running to the altar at the call to repentance. I was kneeling and praying, and, for the first time in my life, I had a woman prophesy over me. I remember she started out praying for me, and then it turned to a prophecy. All I remember hearing was, "You do have the wisdom of God; you will not turn to the right or the left, but you will set your face like flint into the face of God." Boy, oh boy, I left that little church with my spirit filled. I was determined to go back to Tallahassee and find a similar church. Ho, ho, ho! God does go before you.

No sooner had I gotten back to Tallahassee when my friend Lisa from my former spiritual group called me and invited me to a church they were attending. I felt in my spirit that this was the church I was to go into. I started attending every Sunday, and let me tell you, it was like water to a dry and thirsty soul. God led me right into a Holy Spirit-filled full gospel Pentecostal church! The Pastors, Larry and Elaine Millender, were graduates of Rhema Bible College and preached the word of faith, and I was sucking it up.

Even though I was attending church, there was still a lot of the occult influence in me. I was starting a practice as a Naturopath and Master Herbalist out of my house. I would use my pendulum to determine imbalances in a person's body systems. God never said a word, but I do not recall asking either. Some Christians questioned this practice, and some had no problem with it. It showed that the ones who never had a problem did not really know God's word and did not have the discernment of spirits. I did not, so I was no better off.

I was receiving excellent biblical instruction in church, and the eyes of my spirit were starting to open. There were many prophets and healers that visited that little church. Awesome people of faith like Norvell Hayes, Robin and Christian Harfouche, Matt Sorger, Claire Pruitt, and so many others. It was a smorgasbord of spiritual food. I also started attending classes at the Center for Biblical Studies.

I will never forget hearing the testimony of Robin Harfouche when she and her husband spoke at our church. She and Christian operate Global Revival Church in Pensacola, Florida. I remember being riveted to my seat during her testimony. I recall her saying that she had not planned to share her testimony but felt like someone needed to hear it. That someone was me; it was like she was speaking directly to my spirit. You can look up her book From *Hollywood to Heaven* and hear her testimony on YouTube. She was seduced by the occult when she was a young girl, and Hollywood attempted to train her to be another Shirley McClain (whose books I had read!). When she rebelled against those spirits, they tried to kill her. It was radical miraculous divine intervention from God that completely restored her. I got convicted in my spirit that God had intervened in my life to save me from destruction by the occult spirits. At the end of her testimony, she gave an altar call for those who wanted to be free of the occult spirits, and I was one of the firsts to the altar. The eyes of my understanding were opened that day, and I could see the influence of the demonic in my life in a way I had never before. Truly, the veil was torn.

I believe that was the tipping point and the awakening in me of the discernment of spirits. This is a gift of the Holy Spirit, which is not really taught in most of the churches. Thankfully, the Holy Spirit is a teacher and will lead you and guide you. I began to have dreams at a fairly regular interval. The dreams were varied and different, but one thing they had in common. In each dream, I was faced with evil. In one of them, the devil was inside a cabinet. The cabinet was bulging and straining from inside as the evil tried to burst out. I had no fear in any of these dreams; I would just start shouting the name of Jesus. The atmosphere would begin to shift and change, alive with His power, and in all instances, the evil would vanish. I understood that God was teaching me dominion over evil and that the name of Jesus destroyed the darkness, and the evil could not stand.

My Children Suffer from Spiritual Disease

My husband, myself, and Rachael, who was about one year old, went to a retreat in Alabama. It was hosted by the Pentecostal preacher from Australia, who had come to speak at our spiritual group. This retreat comprised all the people who were gravitating towards a more biblical approach. I remember Rob was teaching on healing. He pointed out an area in the mid-torso on an individual who had volunteered. He was asking what people saw in this area and why the healing was not happening. No one (save his wife, who could not tell) said a thing. To me, it was clear as day, so I said, "That spot is like obsidian, it is dark, and the light bounces off, it cannot penetrate. This is what spiritual darkness looks like in the human body. It is where sin abides in the flesh. It comes from the spirit realm, but the thoughts that agree with the sin manifest in the body." Sadly, this was the spot that manifested cancer years later.

I remember when Stan started not feeling well. He came to me for a consultation. I was pretty green in reading the spiritual map, and I was still working with my pendulum (some things take time to get delivered!). I recall being very baffled that every system in his body was reading negative. When he got diagnosed with cancer, I understood why. Although this was a devastating diagnosis, I took it upon myself to be a prayer warrior for him. There was one time when I was laying my hands on him that my eyes were opened, and I "saw" the spirit of cancer. I have to say it was every vile and demonic spirit rolled into one huge mass. I was fascinated and completely repulsed. It was during another time when I was praying for him that I saw the generational spirit of hopelessness and despair that hit his ancestors during a huge drought in California. I had no idea his ancestors were from there, but he confirmed it. We were happy to testify almost a year later that Stan conquered his cancer. It was a battle hard-fought but won. At least on that round. Years later, it came back and took his life. Oh, the victory we will have when one day we can destroy this spiritual wickedness!

I was also baptized in the lake at the retreat by the very same Pentecostal minister I had so strongly rejected the year before. I think God does have a delightful sense of humor.

It was about 2005 when I started taking a course at the Center for Biblical Studies. I took many courses in inner healing, deliverance, and the Father's Love. I learned about the roots of bitterness and the seven spirits under them: unforgiveness, retaliation, revenge, anger, wrath, violence, and murder. I learned about spirits of rejection, envy, jealousy, unclean and unloving spirits, and a whole host more. It was my introduction to spirit world realities and how they gain entrance and wreak havoc on your life.

People, including myself, are like onions, we have many layers of spiritual sickness, and they can only be peeled off a little at a time. You must first recognize that you need healing. If you cannot admit that you need healing, then you will not receive it. So many believe that we are completely healed and delivered when we accept Christ. If this were so, then every Christian would be healed and have no sin in them. Jesus told us, "Heal the sick, cast out demons and raise the dead." He also told us, "I have given you all power over the powers of darkness." This is a sin-filled world, and none of us escapes the stain of sin in our generations. So many of our ancestors worshiped pagan gods and made agreements with the devil. We have the power in the Holy

Spirit to cleanse our generations and cancel generational curses.

One day I was standing in the bookstore at the Center for Biblical Studies when my eyes happened to fall on the book *A More Excellent Way* by Henry Wright. As I bent down to pick up the book, I heard the Lord say, "My children suffer from spiritual disease." I will never forget that moment. It was as if a light went on inside, and I was so intrigued. What did this mean? How could I learn more? Sadly, there was no one to teach this particular subject. I wanted to stay at "Be in Health," Henry Wright's ministry, right then and there, but my husband was not on board.

But the Holy Spirit will have His way. In the meantime, I attended every workshop and course on healing, deliverance, and teachings of the Holy Spirit that was available. Thankfully there were many churches that taught on various gifts and subjects, and I had a smorgasbord to pick from. There was even a school of the Holy Spirit that I attended every Friday night. We had such fun practicing and learning about the gifts of the Holy Spirit.

It was several years later, probably around 2009, when I began to experience pain around my heart area and a numbness that traveled down my left arm. I was no dummy, and with heart disease on both sides of my family, I was seeking the Lord on what to do. I do not go to doctors; I rely on God to heal me. If he saved my life from death, surely, he will deliver me from the snare of the fowler.

A few days later, I received an email from the New Leaf Market, announcing an out-of-town speaker, who claimed she was healed from cancer by God. I was really intrigued, and I asked the Lord if this was someone I should check out in relation to my heart. I felt He was affirming I should go, so I did.

She was a very forceful speaker, and she spoke some of my language about the importance of raw and vibrant foods in the diet. I understood her reference to food having a vibratory force, filled with light, color, and sound. The Holy Spirit had given me dreams and revelation on how color and sound bring healing to the cells of the body. So, I thought this woman had a similar experience with the Lord, and I felt that this was a path to healing my heart through this woman. She was inviting people to a weekend retreat down at her beach house later in the month. I wanted to know more about this, so I invited her to lunch, which she accepted.

We met later that afternoon for lunch, and I was ready with a list of questions about her experience with the Lord concerning her healing. She has glossed over this part, and I was going to zero in.

Unfortunately, from the time we sat down, her entire conversation was "me, me me"—I did this, and I did that. When I asked about God, she started talking about her spirit guides. Oh no, a big red flag! Then I asked her about my heart condition. She looked me dead in the eye and said, "You tell that pain that I said, 'you must stop until you can get down to my retreat at the beach.'"

Oh Lord, this woman knew nothing about Jesus or the Holy Spirit. She was cloaked in darkness, disguising herself as the light. I politely thanked her for having lunch with me and escaped as quickly as possible.

When I got home, I inquired of the Lord as to why he told me to go and listen to her and have lunch together. I immediately saw Deuteronomy 13:1-3 (NIV) in my mind. I looked it up, and it said:

> If a prophet, or one who foretells by dreams, appears among you and announces to you a sign or wonder, and if the sign or wonder spoken of takes place, and the prophet says, "Let us follow other gods and let us worship them," you must not listen to the words of that prophet or dreamer. The Lord your God is testing you to find out whether you love him with all your heart and with all your soul.

I was floored! He did that on purpose so that I would know the difference between the true and false spirits. God is really good, and that is not just a saying: He brings you the teaching and training you need, at the time you need it.

It had now been two years since I had wanted to attend the "Be in Health" ministry. It was about a week after this incidence when my husband walked out of the bedroom with the book *A More Excellent Way* by Henry Wright. He looked at me and said, "I think we need to go here." You could have knocked me over with a feather! This sort of comment never comes out of my husband. I knew God was speaking through him.

I made arrangements the next day for our one-week stay at "Be in Health" in Thomaston, Georgia. The entire family was going. Hannah was only five years old, and they required you to be at least six, but I convinced them that she was a mature five-year-old. I was so excited; I just knew that this was an important step in furthering my knowledge of how the spirit realm impacts the physical body.

We had a nice cabin to stay in while we spent the week at "Be in Health." The children went for their own ministry, and Dennis and I were in class from eight to five every day and had homework at night. Each day focused on different spirits and how they influence our thoughts. Those thoughts then influence the physical body as they travel down the limbic (or emotional system), and depending on your genetic inheritance, will target the weakest systems. For example, the spirit of fear: most people and even Christians do not realize that this is an actual living demon. It is very real, and its job is to destroy your life in a variety of ways. I remember how shocked I was to learn that all these spirits were real, alive, and eternally destined to destroy our life. To say it was an eye-opener is an understatement!

I learned that once we are made aware of how these spirits influence our thoughts, then it is our job to repent of cooperating with them and renounce them in our lives. Luke 11:24-25 says, "When the unclean spirit has gone out of a man, he walks through the dry places, seeking rest; and finding none, he says I will return to my house where I came out. When it arrives, it finds the house swept clean and put in order" (my rephrase).

This is a very important scripture as it tells us that once the demon has been cast out, he will roam around looking for a place to rest, and finding none, he will come back to you. The house (your mind, your spirit) is now clean of its evil influence, and he says, "I will go into this house and bring some friends with me."

So, what prevents these spirits from returning? It is and always will be the Word of God. Only Spirit trumps a spirit. You cannot fight spiritual evil with your intellect. Those spirits only listen to one voice, and that is the living word. It is the sword of the Spirit, the word of God.

All deliverance ministry at "Be in Health" is done in a large group setting. There is an all-day teaching of how these spirits influence your thoughts. That is why Satan is called the prince of the air: he works to get you to agree with him in your thoughts, and then your health will follow.

It was Wednesday, and we had been in class since Monday morning. Today was the teaching on the spirit of rejection. Rejection is a form of self-idolatry, not believing that God loves you, holding on to what man thinks of you. This was a major button pusher for me; I was sucking up the knowledge of how this spirit influences people because I knew that this was the main spirit in my family line. My father was rejected by his father, and my mother was rejected by her father. I felt rejected by both my parents. How is a child to know God loves them if God is not in the home? In the group prayer of deliverance from this spirit, I felt the pain leave my heart. It was tangible, and it has never returned.

Looking back, I see how God allowed me to believe it was His will (actually because it was) to go and listen to the woman who claimed God healed her cancer, when in fact, she was working with false spirits. Now He put me in a place to see and experience the power of His Holy Spirt over the power of darkness. Did Jesus not say, "Behold, I have given you authority to tread upon serpents and scorpions, and over all power of the enemy: and nothing shall in any wise hurt you" (Luke 10:19 ASV)? It is not enough to read the scriptures; you must experience the very living word.

There were several other spirits delivered; bitterness and all the seven spirits that come under bitterness: unforgiveness, revenge, retaliation, anger, wrath, violence, and murder (including murder with the tongue). There were also occult spirits that were dealt with. I got a holy conviction from the Lord about using my pendulum, and I went home and tossed it out.

It was a marvelous and eye-opening experience into the reality of the spirit world. Most people in America have no idea this realm exists, even the church. The early church laid hands on the sick and cast out demons, but the father of all lies taught that these powers were of the past, and this sort of thing does not happen anymore. Wake up, Church! These powers of the Holy Spirit are alive and operating in those that believe. Meanwhile, the devil is going unchecked. Look at the chaos that is in America right now. Anarchy in the streets! The demonic release of a deadly virus. We must take up the Sword of the Spirit and start operating in the power Christ died to give us.

Practicing Healing and Deliverance

I received my Doctor of Naturopathy and Master Herbalist degree from Trinity College of Natural Health in 1997. It was not until 2002 that I began to practice out of my home in Tallahassee. The former years were just too turbulent, and life settled down after Rachael was born.

I remember the early years when I would travel to people's homes, do my kinesiology with my pendulum (before "Be in Health"), go home and work out which herbs would best suit the customer. It was a lot of labor with few results. I would pray and pray for enlightenment, for knowledge and wisdom, and slowly but surely, God has granted those prayers. First, I got rid of the pendulum. Second, I opened up an office in my home. I was then stuck with the question of how to discern patterns of weakness in the body without my crutch. I recall discussing this with God, and one day He clearly said, "Listen to my Holy Spirit." Frankly, I was petrified. How was I to hear the voice of God?

I would touch specific what we call "test points" (corresponding to organs, minerals, vitamins, etc.) on a person's body, close my eyes and try to discern what the Holy Spirit was saying. It turned out I was hearing him the whole time; I just did not recognize this because I was so focused on the pendulum. I began to discover that God would give me pictures in my mind and words of what was happening in a person's body. For example, I might touch the liver, and I would see a picture of either a fatty liver or it would appear hard. I would tap the adrenals and understand that this person had adrenal exhaustion. This was by no means an easy process; I struggled a lot with believing what I was hearing. The Holy Spirit does not diagnose like the medical society. He paints pictures and gives words as to the overall state of the person's body. So, you do not look at the disease the same way in Naturopathy. I look at the whole state. Much like a house that is cluttered and full of garbage, you do a systematic cleaning, room by room, or body system by body system, until the whole house is clean and shiny.

Along with the gift of knowledge came the gift of discernment of generational spirits that had come down the line along with more common spirits of fear, bitterness, envy, jealousy, etc. I had taken many classes in deliverance ministry, and it was something that I have a gift for. Jesus did command us to "cast out demons," did he not? I took him up on the authority he has given us.

I would pray and command them to leave and ask the Holy Spirit to bring a cleansing back down the generational line, all the way from Adam. Most importantly, you must teach the person to fill their mind with scripture so that the "thought demon" does not return. Much of this, I do with more ease these days, but there is always a struggle to discern what or if negative spirits are impacting the health.

When I opened my home office, one of my first clients was a beautiful black woman named Desiree. She came with a diagnosis of Hepatitis C that she was seeking natural treatment for. She was one of the first recipients of my Holy Spirit prayer work. God had just told me to start praying with my customers. There are some people who have it in their spirit to be a sponge and soak up every bit of spirit power available, and this woman was one of them. We started praying, and it might have been a Sunday service at a full gospel church. The presence was powerful. Here was a woman who had a rich African heritage and powerful tribal leaders in her heritage. There was a strong presence of witchcraft and voodoo that was against her and her calling. I used deliverance ministry to deal with the ancestral witchcraft and the voodoo spirit. Jesus always trumps evil, and there was a victory for this fine lady.

There were also lesions on her liver that I saw in the spirit. She confirmed that an MRI showed abnormal, hard tissue on her liver in three spots. I recommended antiviral herbs such as olive leaf, astragalus root, and echinacea. We also used liver cleansing herbs such as milk thistle, burdock root, yellow dock, and barberry. It took a year, but all viral loads came back within the normal range, and the lesions on the liver started shrinking. Today there is no longer the presence of Hepatitis or liver problems, and she is fulfilling her calling as a dynamic leader of her church.

One of my favorite clients was Jacob. He came to me seeking help for adrenal exhaustion. He had already been to medical doctors, naturopaths, and chiropractic doctors and had not gotten any better. I remember he asked me, "Do you think there is any hope?"

I replied, "Jacob, with God, all things are possible." I truly believe that the Creator of this vast universe and everything in it can create or uncreate at will.

Jacob was a lapsed Catholic. He grew up in a very large family and went to the Catholic church and school. Like most, he turned away from his faith because he got a whole lot of religion but never had a personal encounter with Jesus. He also did not want much to do with God. I fought tirelessly with that spirit of the anti-

Christ in Jacob. I prayed for him at every opportunity, I read him scripture and told him who he was in Christ. I had my work cut out for me. It is much easier when a person has a good relationship with the Lord, but it is not a requirement; otherwise, Jesus would have never had healed anyone.

I remember our very first prayer session. I told Jacob that I was going to pray and ask the Holy Spirit if there were any spiritual roadblocks to his recovery. I had no sooner started praying when the Lord showed me three demons that were hovering over Jacob. They were fear, torment, and death. I bound these spirits and broke their power over Jacob's life. You could feel the atmosphere change. I asked him about this after we were done, and he told me that the night after they buried his father, he woke up in terror and saw these demons over his bed! These generational spirits travel on down the line from father to son upon the father's death. Once these spirits were gone, Jacob started to recover. Today he has completely recovered his health.

I said that I had prayed for Jacob tirelessly. I read scripture to him, prayed for him every time he came, and encouraged him to have a deeper relationship with God, but he was not budging. I was talking to God one day before Jacob's monthly appointment, and I said, "God, I don't think I can help him anymore; I have gone as far as I can. Do I have your permission to tell him this?" I got an instant, "no." I was to keep on praying for him and to keep on encouraging him to have a closer walk with God. With God, obedience is of the utmost importance. I learned from the start: you just do it. The blessings will follow later.

It was about six months later when Jacob came into my office quite excited. He told me something spectacular had happened! Wow, was I curious! I urged him to tell me from the beginning.

He said that every day he would talk out loud to God, and he would say, "If you're real, show me, heal me." Then he would say, "Oh, just forget about it" (the impatient child!). Well, one time, he prayed the prayer but did not say forget about it. He was lying on his bed when the room began to fill with light, it was full of all colors of the rainbow, and a beautiful presence filled his room. The energy in the room was so powerful that he began to rise off his bed. Simultaneously with this, the light beams began to shoot into his body. He said they looked like geometric prisms of light, and he knew that they were healing his emotions. He had no fear, just awe and wonder. Jacob said he knew it was God, and he was content that God knew who he was and that He was real.

It is amazing to me the gifts and strategies God uses to woo his children. It had to be something so out of the box, so extraordinary that it would captivate Jacob's spirit! God is so awesome!

In another instance, a woman came to me for help with uterine fibroids. As I prayed, I heard the Holy Spirit reveal some specific information. I stopped praying and very gently asked this woman if she had ever been raped. She tearfully replied that she had been raped not once but twice. I prayed that this door of trauma would be closed, and I helped her release feelings of guilt, shame, fear, and unforgiveness. Once the trauma and associated spirits were dealt with, I coached her to begin speaking God's Word to herself. In the months to follow, those fibroids started to shrink. I also recommended herbs to help clean and tone the uterus, along with hormone-balancing herbs. In healing, we need to address the spirit, but we also need to support the physical body as it heals.

The years in Tallahassee were years of training: learning patience, obedience, learning to clear my own spirit of rejection, bitterness, and the occult. We are all a work in progress, but we have to be willing to work, to examine ourselves, and ask the Lord where the dark areas are so He can shed His light. Often, we are not aware of our darkness, for the darkness likes to hide. We need to be willing to let our brothers and sisters minister to us by the Holy Spirit. The more is light that shines in the darkness, the freer you become. You can become unoffendable and free from fear and worry. This is the joy that Jesus died to give us.

Moving to My Next Assignment

In 2007, my father died. He spent his life as a metallurgical engineer. He worked with special metal paints and was one of the first to train at Alcoa in Tennessee in their new program. The toxic metal cost him his life as he was struck with a slow form of leukemia. He was an advocate of alternative medicine and had IV chelation therapy done several times. My father would not speak of God. If you tried to talk to him about God, he would get very angry. He was never able to stop drinking, and this contributed to his heart disease and kidney failure. He kept saying that he was going to die. The Word warns, "For the thing which I greatly fear comes upon me, and that of which I am afraid has come upon me" (Job 3:25 AMP).

It is true—what we speak becomes our reality. Without the Word of God and the Spirit of God in my father's life, he was controlled by generational bitterness, rejection, and addiction. He fared better than his only brother, who became an alcoholic and lost his family, job, home, and life. "The thief comes only to steal, kill, and destroy" (John 10:10 NIV). Without Jesus, who said, "I have given you authority to tread on serpents and scorpions and over all power of the enemy" (Luke 10:19 NASB), we become victims instead of victors.

As my father lay dying on his hospital bed, I was interceding in the spirit. I prayed in tongues for three hours. I asked for mercy and forgiveness for his rejection of God.

My father was in a drug-induced coma at the end of his life. Whether he heard me praying (and I think he did) or not, I will never know until I get to heaven. In the third hour, I felt a shift in the atmosphere and sensed the presence of angels and the Holy Spirit. It was very powerful; I began to weep. I knew Jesus had offered His hand to my father, and he took it. In my mind's eye, I saw the angels wrap his spirit in their huge wings and take him away. God is so much more merciful than we give him credit. He truly desires and declares, "And I give them eternal life, and they will never, ever perish, and no one will ever snatch them out of my hand" (John 10:28 AMP).

My mother had been diagnosed with Alzheimer's a few years prior to my dad's passing. At his death, she went into a downward spiral for the next few years. The night he died, she was overcome by the spirit of abandonment. She was so full of fear she had dry heaves. My sister and I got up and prayed for her, but this fear would leave her in bondage until the end. This spirit came into her life when her own father walked out of the marriage when she was nine years old. Her mother was also abandoned as an infant. My grandmother's mother died of tuberculosis shortly after she was born, and her father could not face raising her on his own, so she was given to his sister to raise. Here on both sides of her family line were rejection and abandonment. When my father died, and her source of strength and security left, those spirits came to plague her.

The spirit of rejection is the one that whispers in your ear that you will never be loved, that everyone you love will leave you. The response is that the child walls off their heart and cannot let anyone in. Divorce may be the result, as you purposely (but unconsciously) push away those you love. Or you may not be able to be completely intimate with your spouse.

Interestingly enough, there is always confirmation in the scriptures. John 4:18 (AKJV): "There is no fear in love; but perfect love casts out all fear: because fear has torment." Here we see insanity (Alzheimer's) coming out of rejection. Rejection confuses the mind and intellect or provokes double-mindedness.

Rejection looks for identity outside of Christ. This is why it is called an identity crisis. This person then will find another friend, mentor, or spouse to tell them who they are. Without my father to give my mother her identity, she fell apart. This is by no means a cut and dried ministry. We in the western world would like to find and pinpoint one cause or remedy and presto—be healed and done with it. It is just not so.

I have also discovered that candida overgrowth plays a big role in Alzheimer's. My mother had chronic diarrhea for over ten years. She went to five different gastroenterologists and never got well. One medication they put her on caused her to wander naked out of her condominium with a sheet wrapped around her. She was not that far gone at that point that this was caused by her Alzheimer's, rather it was a disastrous side effect of the medication. After my dad died and I started caring for her more, I took her off all grains and sugar. She had started drinking white wine (the really sweet stuff), so that had to go. All she was eating was carbohydrates. I put her on meat and vegetables. I gave her bentonite clay and turkey rhubarb to dry up the diarrhea, probiotics, and herbs like chaparral, pad arco, and calendula to combat the yeast. The diarrhea cleared up in a few weeks. Such a shame that doctors ignore natural remedies. It is said that Alzheimer's is the diabetes of the brain; this could very well be true.

God also showed me something else as a root of her affliction. My grandfather was a Mason who also died of Alzheimer's. He came from a long line of Masons from Scotland. The Lord told me to rebuke, repent, and renounce the curse on my family line, which I did. This secret brotherhood has its roots in much of American culture. Many of our Founding Fathers were Masons.

Interestingly enough, when my grandfather died, my mother gave me a box of his things. In an envelope were his Mason Degree, his ring, and other masonic items. I was not even born in the spirit at that point, yet I was repulsed by these things, and I threw them in the trash. How fascinating that my spirit knew they were evil, even when I had no knowledge.

In a similar fashion, I burned an ancestral Swedish Crest that was made by my great great great grandmother. I repented and renounced all familiar spirits that came down the line, set that Crest on fire, and literally burned up the generational sin. My father slept under that crest. It was a framed picture over his side of the bed. Imagine the head of an eagle with malice in his eyes and a tongue forked with fire. It made me shudder to look at it. Those Vikings were some fierce people.

When it became apparent that my mother could no longer live alone around 2011, my sister and I took turns going down to Palm Beach to care for her. One of us would have to agree to care for her until the end, and

I would not put my mother in a home. My sister said she just could not do it, so that left me. Thankfully, my husband was fine with that.

Since our house in Tallahassee was too small to accommodate her, it was decided that my mother would provide the funds, and we would move to another house. Dennis and I had wanted to move up around North Carolina or Tennessee in the mountains, so here was our chance. Little did I know God was about to put me on the ride of a lifetime!

We were looking for a house with acreage that was backed up to or near federal or state land. We wanted a homestead. My sister, who was the trustee and had a power of attorney, was allowing a certain amount of money for this, so our budget was not huge for five people. Everywhere were looked, it was either too expensive, too small, or too dilapidated. I was ferociously praying to God to show us where we should go. I knew that only He would know where we would prosper.

I discussed different places with my sister and told her nothing was looking good. I remember she said, "What about South Carolina?" I replied, "I would never move to South Carolina." Never say never. It seems like that is a dare to God!

One day I was having my morning coffee, praying and talking to God around the second week of February 2012. I had just sat down with my second cup of coffee when the atmosphere began to shift. It was as if a cloud came down through the ceiling and was hovering over me. It seemed to settle over my head. I felt like Moses on Mount Sinai. All I could do was weep; the presence of God was completely overwhelming. Two words came out of that cloud. It felt like they were dropped deep in my spirit. I could feel them as if they were alive! Those words were "Kings Mountain!" This visitation lasted only a minute, but it had such a profound effect on me. I knew that God had spoken, and He was directing us to move to Kings Mountain, wherever that was.

I immediately went online and googled it. Kings Mountain, North Carolina, was the first to come up. I was excited and called my husband and told him all that had happened. Yes, I was met with doubt, but that did not bother me; my husband does not exactly share my enthusiasm sometimes. I started looking for houses in Kings Mountain, but absolutely nothing came up, and I became very frustrated. I was sure the perfect house would show itself immediately.

After a few hours of searching, I then broadened my search to within twenty-five miles of Kings Mountain. Suddenly up popped this one house, set in the woods, with a large wrap around porch, ten acres, a barn, lake, and an in-ground pool. I switched to google maps to see it, and when I did, the Holy Spirit flooded me with goosebumps. That house was in South Carolina (where

I would never move), sitting at the base of Kings Mountain State Park, where the battle of Kings Mountain was fought and won during the revolutionary war. Even now, as I write this, I get those same goosebumps. I knew without any doubt that this was the house we had been looking for. It did not matter that the price was 50,000 higher than our budget or that it was listed as a short sale. God can move through those obstacles.

My husband and I put in an offer, and I have to say, looking back, that the offer was ridiculously low. I believe a spirit of pride was operating, as we thought God was just going to give it to us on a silver platter. Three days later, we were notified that our offer was rejected. We decided that we would drive up there and look at the house and land. The night before we were to leave, we got a call from our realtor. He told us the house was under contract and was not being shown. Talk about devastation! We were emotionally and spiritually crushed. Did I get this all wrong? Did I not hear from God? What was going on?

My husband grilled me over and over about what God said. I became defensive and angry. I knew I heard His voice, and I knew that it was to be our house, so what went wrong? I called my friends Stan and Lisa. Lisa has a seer anointing and can see very clearly in the spirit realm, and Stan always has wisdom and insight from the Lord. I valued and needed their insight. I told them what had transpired, and I asked them to pray with me. I recall as we were talking on the phone, Lisa suddenly said, "something huge has entered the atmosphere." I do not see like she does, but I hear, and I heard that an Angel of the Lord was present to usher in Jesus's presence. I could see Jesus with my spiritual eyes, and His presence is one of authority and perfect peace. Over the next few seconds, He told me that He was giving me His Faith to stand for the house. It did not matter who was against me; His faith would see me through. His presence gave me so much peace over the situation and confidence that He was with me and fighting for me.

I told my husband what Jesus had told me. In April, over Easter weekend, we decided that we would drive up there and camp at Kings Mountain State Park. We would drive by and look at the house. I had told my sister what was going on, and since, to the natural eye, it did not look like we were going to get the house, she suggested maybe there was another house in the area. When nothing goes as you think it should, it is very easy to be swayed by an unbeliever!

When we turned onto the dirt road where the house was, we just sat there in the car, almost afraid to go out and have a look at the house. We had looked at pictures of the house online a thousand times, yet here it was in the flesh, so to speak, and we so desperately wanted that house. My husband always joked that he knew it was God because everything about the house was what I told him I did not want. Before the Lord spoke, I had my list: there would be no renovations, I wanted an updated kitchen and baths, etc., and here was this house that needed major renovations in the kitchen and the bathrooms!

I loved it anyway! The beauty of the property was exquisite.

We decided to drive around and see if there was any other property for sale. In the previous months, I would sit with the Lord in the morning, having my coffee and talking with Him. My mind would wander, and I would have this repeated vision: in my imaginings, there was this little old lady standing out on the end of her driveway by the mailbox. There was a for sale sign on her property. She invited me and my husband and children inside her house; then she gave us her house to live in. I would always shake my head and tell myself this was silly and to get back to my prayers.

While we were driving along all the roads that border the park, my husband started telling me about a dream he had the night before. He told me that in the dream, there was this little old lady standing out on the road by her mailbox. Her house was for sale, and she invited us in along with my mother; she and my mother became good friends, and she ended up giving us the house. He was telling me this dream, and I was sitting there in shocked silence with the hair standing up on my head. I then told him about my morning visions, and we were driving around, wondering what this meant.

I was convinced God had a message here, and Dennis thought it was just a coincidence. There is *no* coincidence with God! So here we were, driving around, looking for a little old lady that was standing on the road beside her mailbox. It was crazy, and, of course, we never saw the old lady, but that vision did come to pass years later, when my mother passed away and the trust paid off the house.

We went back to Tallahassee, determined to do whatever it takes to get that house; however, it was under contract. On Mother's Day in May, I decided to take the next step of faith, packed up my two girls, and moved down to Palm Beach to take care of my mom and get her house ready to sell. In my determination, I called the realtor every two weeks and ask if the house was still under contract. He thought I was crazy when I told him God wanted me to have that house, but who cares! The only thing that mattered was getting the house and pursuing what the Lord had said. I repeatedly told the realtor when the guy walked away, would he please call me.

Months went by, and I was overwhelmed at the task of selling my mom's belongings and packing up what I wanted the movers to take. My sister was listening to her friends and was convinced that I was being influenced by the devil. She said to me, "Why would God give you a house, ten acres, a barn, and a pool?" Apparently, I was not worthy of this in her eyes. Needless to say, we did not speak much.

I was in a faith battle, and I had no one but God on my side. My husband would call and say, "Are we really moving?" I had to boost both of our faiths, and it was draining. I would confess the Word every day, especially when the devil started attacking my belief that I would not get the house. I would pace the house and confess the word out loud. I specifically stood on a scripture that the Lord gave me in the beginning.

Isaiah 43 was my scripture, and I mean the entire chapter. Various parts of it such as 43:1 (NASB): "Do not fear, for I have redeemed you; I have called you by name; you are Mine! When you pass through the waters, I will be with you; And through the rivers, they will not overflow you. When you walk through the fire, you will not be scorched, Nor will the flame burn you" I also stood on Isaiah 43:18-19 (AMP): "Do not remember the former things, Or ponder the things of the past. Listen carefully, I am about to do a new thing. Now it will spring forth; Will you not be aware of it?" The entire chapter and the various verses became my living water. I battled doubt and fear daily, but I took up the sword of the spirit, the Word of God, and defeated the enemy daily.

It was during that summer of 2012 that I began to look at the way I was coping, with all the stress of moving to my mother's, leaving my husband behind in Tallahassee, and standing in faith for a house that looked impossible in the natural world. My lifelong answer to fear (which is worry, anxiety) and conflict was to have a beer or a glass of wine every night and always more than one. I knew I had an addiction, and I knew I had to do something about it.

I had started attending Christ Fellowship in Palm Beach Gardens, and it was through there that I saw a program for addictions. I called the number and was immediately connected with a group where I could get insight and help. It was different from AA. This Christian group focused on the various childhood traumas and conflicts that happened in my early years. The emotional scars that I carried caused me to turn to the generational spirit of addiction. For instance, I learned that children of alcoholics are often neat freaks (like I am) because they could not control their chaotic environment in childhood, so cleaning their surroundings and making everything neat and perfect gives them a sense of control. I felt that as a child, I was not valued or honored for just being me. As a child, I was to be seen and not heard. My opinions and voice were not honored, but squashed. I was not given much encouragement for any individuality, I was lectured and told, "This is the way it is going to be." This led to feelings of insecurity in my own decision making and feelings of worthlessness. I was a very fearful and timid child and as an adolescent and young adult. I covered the fear and insecurity with drugs and alcohol as they have a marvelous way of making you forget your troubles and give you a false sense of courage.

I had a deep fear of failure, I was terribly insecure in making my decisions, and I had a rebellious spirit. When you have rules without a relationship, it can lead to rebellion. I rebelled, and my sister conformed to perfectionism. I was also prey to the Judgmental and Critical spirit that came down from my father's line. This spirit finds fault with everything and anyone, so no one will look to you. It serves as a shield to hide your own fear of failure.

I suffered extreme panic attacks as a teenager. I had so much fear, and I had no idea of who I was in Christ. As God started exposing the generational sins and curses in my family line, it opened my eyes to the baggage I was carrying and how I was coping with it. I believe that in Christ, we do not cope, we overcome. We examine the dysfunctional patterns and the spirits that come with them, and then we repent of cooperating with them one by one. We must then declare what God says about us in scripture. If Christ died on the cross to break the power of guilt, shame, rejection, and many other sins, then we must, by the power of the Holy Spirit, appropriate what He has done for us. We must take action. We cannot sit and say, "Well, if God wants me free, He will set me free," or, "This was all done when I accepted Jesus in my life." While this is the belief of many, years of ministry and my own deliverance from afflicting and generational spirits says otherwise.

It is the freedom from sin that builds the health of the mind, the body, and the spirit. It must start in the spirit and come down into the body. In the alternative healing practices today it is all focused on what we put into the body. But did not Jesus say in Mark 7:15 (AMP), "There is nothing outside a man which by going into him can defile him, but the things which come out of the heart of a man are what defile and dishonor him"?

There was another battle during my faith walk for the house, and that was forgiveness. My husband had repeated doubts, and I had to forgive him for not believing that this was God's will over and over. My sister was the biggest battle. She repeatedly came against me and tried to sabotage my faith. First, it was that I was listening to the devil and not God. The second battle was when I finally got that phone call I had been waiting for!

In the middle of September, the realtor I had been speaking with for the past five months finally called. He said these words that I will never forget, "I don't know what happened, but we can't find the guy who has the contract on the house." I was elated! I was in shock; I was ecstatic! I told him we would be putting in a bid later that day. I called my husband and my sister. We knew that the other buyer had recently counter-offered the bank a certain amount, so we were prepared to put in slightly above that. I was finally rejoicing that we would have victory over this situation, and then the realtor called back.

The other guy came back! No, this could not be happening! God, this is not fair! *Why are you doing this to me, God? And now we had to bid against him! Was he going to bid the same amount? Was he going to go higher? Help, Jesus!*

Those were exactly the thoughts running through my mind. I thank goodness my husband is always calm when I am in a crisis. We decided on an amount slightly higher than what the other guy had counter-offered the bank the last time.

We got the call the next day. We got the bid! Hallelujah, we finally got the house; the wait was over!

But *no*! Three days later the realtor called and said Freddy Mac (remember it was a short sale) threw out the bid. They would not sell to my mother's trust. The reasoning behind this was that if there ever is a foreclosure, Freddy Mac cannot foreclose on an entity, only a person.

To say that my husband and I were devastated was an understatement—I just could not understand what was happening and why they were happening this way. I felt as if I had no control over anything, and I believe that this is by God's infinite wisdom. I was reeling and feeling hopeless and just a bit mad at God. Why was this happening? I just did not understand. My sister, who controlled the finances, told me that she never wanted to hear about this house again. She told me to look for something else. I am pretty sure I hung up on her.

If there is ever something that raises the spirit of rebellion in me, it is being told what I can and cannot do!

I kept thinking of this scripture: "So will My word be which goes out of My mouth; It will not return to be void, without accomplishing what I desire, and without succeeding in the matter for which I sent it" (Isaiah 55:11 AMP). God had spoken, and His word would not return void.

I called my husband to discuss what we should do. I have to give him credit: when my faith is at its rock bottom, he rallies. He told me my sister was not in charge of our future. We decided that we would put in our own bid for the house, in our names...and we had no money.

The next day I got to work. I went up to the bank and asked them if they would draft me a letter showing the amounts in the account. The letter was not to state that it was my mother's money, only that the cash was there. The woman at the bank agreed to do this for me. One down. I then called Mitch, who was in charge of my mother's investments. My sister and I had flown up to Pittsburgh the year before and personally met with him, so he knew me. I asked him to do the same as I had asked the bank, and he agreed. I then called the realtor and put in a bid for the house. The next day the realtor told me they accepted our offer. Wonderful, we got the contract, but now the reality was, we had no money to buy the house.

Dennis and I and the girls decided to drive up and look at the house, now that we had it under contract. We all loved it, even with all the repairs it needed. The land was gorgeous. While we were there, the neighbors came over and introduced themselves. We told them we were going to buy the house, and they invited us over to swim and have a beer, I was still drinking, but my husband does not drink. I thought the neighbors were wonderful! I had been praying for good neighbors and to have a friend. For some reason, Dennis did not get the same warm fuzzy feeling I did. We left and drove back to Florida, wondering what was going to happen. The girls and I went back down to my mom's, and I began to sweat bullets.

Every night and probably all through the day, I would be asking God what we were going to do, *Could he please talk to me and tell me what to do? Could he please give some clues? Could he please rescue me out of this situation? How am I going to get this house?*

To make matters worse, I was not speaking to my sister, and she was desperate to know what was going on. She spoke to the finance company and found out I asked for the letter. The next thing I know, she pulled all my mother's money and put it in another account. Good golly! Did she think I was going to just take my mother's money? We were at odds once again.

A month went by, and nothing happened about the house. I was afraid to call the realtor, afraid he might ask for money. I was beyond sweating bullets; it was now blood. I was quoting scripture and the promises of God morning, noon, and night. If I did not, the enemy called fear would hijack me.

Then at the beginning of September, I got a text message from our new neighbor up in South Carolina. She sent me a picture of a foreclose sign on the front door of my house. What the heck? What was going on?

I called my realtor, who did not even know it had gone into foreclosure. I called the number on the fore-closure sign and talked with a very nice lady who told me that a law firm was holding the title. I explained to her that I had been trying to buy this house for almost a whole year. She told me there should not be a problem with the trust, and she would call me right back. She called me back and said the sweetest words I would ever hear, "There is no problem with your mother's trust purchasing the house." Hallelujah, all over again! Now the only problem was I had not spoken to my sister in over a month.

So, I texted her and told her what was going on. Thank God for texting; it is the chicken way out.

I have to shout a Hallelujah to my sister; she got on the phone and went to bat! There is a little (although this was a huge disappointment and betrayal) side note here. Originally, my sister was to give cash for the sale of the house. At the last minute, she decided to mortgage the house. This was not the original agreement, and I felt very betrayed. I remember speed walking the neighborhood, screaming at God, asking him over and over why I was getting shafted again and again throughout this whole process.

Naturally, I never got an answer, and I had to just tell God over and over again that I forgave my sister. I knew I could not let bitterness have one foot in the door. Genesis 4:7 (AMP): "If you do well (believing Me and doing what is acceptable and pleasing Me), will you not be accepted? And if you do not do well (but ignore My instruction), sin crouches at your door; its desire is for you, but you must master it." God says, "For if you forgive others their trespasses, your heavenly Father will also forgive you" (Mathew 6:14 ESV). I know I always have to be quick to forgive. If unforgiveness takes hold, then bitterness follows. So many do not understand that unforgiveness and bitterness are the roots of their disease. Bitterness carries seven spirits with it, and it will eat away at your physical body.

We were running into a problem with the banks: no one wanted to lend the money for the sale of the house. We literally had 48 hours to find a bank before the realtor put the house on the market; she was giving us grace! I professed the word over and over that day and late into the next, but fear was creeping up on me. Then at the last minute, it was almost 5:00 p.m., and banks were closing, my sister found a bank that would lend the money. Hooray, I was doing the victory dance! We called the realtor and set the paperwork in motion.

I was hoping that for my fifty-second birthday, I would get the gift of having all the paperwork done and a date for the signing, but it did not happen. It was my 12/12/12 birthday year: I was expecting great things, and God did not disappoint. Shortly after, I got the word that the house was ours. You cannot imagine the tears of joy that I had. It was such an intense yearlong battle.

I end up going up and signing the papers in Gaffney, South Carolina, on February 4, 2013, exactly a year after God spoke those words, "Kings Mountain."

The Next Battle

You would think the after all the chaos of the previous year, I would find some rest from tribulation, but apparently, that was not in God's plan.

First, I had to take care of my mother, whose Alzheimer's got progressively worse after the move. This is to be expected with the disease, but the reality is a whole different ball game.

After living through this, I can honestly say that I believe this is demonic possession. My mother was raised with religion but never met Jesus. I think fear is a real root in this disease, that and generational sin. She would talk to people she saw in the mirror, and she would sometimes be mean and violent. If I anointed the doors, mirrors, and her pillow, there would be some peace from all such outbursts, but they would come back twenty-four hours later. It was a constant and unrelenting battle. I feel for everyone who has to take care of a loved one with this curse.

She also had times when she was really sweet. My mom was a fantastic swimmer, but with this disease, she forgot how. I would get her in the pool and wrap noodles around her so she could float. That would sometimes bring her joy, and sometimes she could not get over her fear of not knowing how to swim. My daughter Hannah, who was only nine at the time, has a special gift for the elderly and babies. She would take my mother by the hand and ask her if she wanted to watch a movie. This brought my mom such delight, like a small child. They watched endless movies together, and my mother was so calm in her presence.

I will never forget when she was having a fairly lucid day. She looked at me, and I knew my real mother was back, but she had such torment in her eyes. Her voice trembled in anguish when she looked at me imploringly and said, "help me, what is happening to me?" She was screaming for help in there, and I was powerless to do anything. I gently explained that she had some memory problems, and just like that, she was gone, never to return.

There were many times day and night I would clean up her messes, I would be showering her off or cleaning her bottom, and she would be hitting me, telling me to leave her alone. She did not know who I was. To get through this, I would say under my breath, "Jesus, this is my mother and your daughter, I love her, and I will serve her. Bless her, Jesus." I had to remind myself that she was God's child, and I was doing this for Him. His word says, "Honor (respect, obey, care for) your father and your mother" (Exodus 20:12 AMP); this is the first commandment with a promise. My mother did not have her own mind anymore; it was controlled by darkness. My job was to simply take care of her the best I could without resentment, murmuring, or complaining. Yes, that was hard, and I had to repent of my thoughts and actions many times.

On New Year's Eve in 2014, she fell and broke her hip. She recovered from the surgery but slowly went downhill from there. She eventually passed away in a beautiful Hospice Center a month later.

During that first year, those lovely neighbors of ours showed their true colors.

It all started when Dennis went around our ten acres to find all of the boundary markers. When he came to the border of our house and the neighbors, the marker was absent. They had installed a shed right before we moved in, and it appeared to be on our property. When we were at their house before we moved up there, they had told us that they owned part of the lake, and they did have their canoes and chairs down there. Unfortunately for them, we had the plat to the property, and we knew they did not own part of our lake, and as a matter of fact, our boundary went halfway up their back yard. So, Dennis hired a surveyor to map out the boundary.

Apparently, the neighbors watched our house closely, as no sooner had the experts surveyed the boundary when the neighbors came charging out, screaming all sorts of obscenities to my husband and the survey team. It was totally out of the left field and quite a shocker. I had no idea of the hatred these people had for anyone who they perceived to cross them. We were in our rights, but not in their eyes. We were challenging their lies, and they did not like it. And that was what set off the war, only it was a one-sided war, for we refused to participate.

For two years, they screamed obscenities at us, played loud music, shot guns, and at one point, had a loudspeaker sending off an alarm at 3 a.m., 5 a.m., etc. They sat and plotted their perceived revenge. Psalm 37: 10-15 is one I have stood on and recited many times:

> A little while and the wicked will be no more; though you look for them, they will not be found. But the meek will inherit the land and enjoy peace and prosperity. The wicked plot against the righteous and gnash their teeth at them; but the Lord laughs at the wicked, for he knows their day is coming.
>
> Psalm 37: 10-15 (NIV)

I have never in my life experienced such hatred and evil. My husband and I knew that we could never ever say anything to them or retaliate in any way. Let me tell you, it is hard to turn the other cheek. We did call the police for harassment, and she was arrested, but that did not seem to stop them. It is extremely difficult to live in peace when there is a spirit of bitterness constantly bombarding you. It was a very tough lesson in restraint.

I recall one time I was out in our lake on my paddleboard, and the neighbors were up on their balcony, with their adult children, drinking beer. When they saw me, the wife began calling me obscene and vulgar names. She was goading her husband to join. I felt horribly naked, exposed, and attacked under their evil. But God had another idea to use this evil for His good. He told me to paddle over, so I was standing (on my board) directly down the hill and under their attack. I was shaking and afraid, but I just obeyed what I felt the Lord saying. I stood under their barrage of bitterness. Their son came down from the porch and started shooting his gun at the target, literally ten feet from me.

I stood my ground and began to speak scripture. Not loudly, just in a normal voice. The Word is a powerful weapon against the enemy. I remember saying, "Lord, like a dog returning to its own vomit, let them turn and rend themselves." I spoke many passages of scripture and stood my ground. Within minutes they broke out fighting amongst themselves, with the adults shouting at each other and the children storming off in their vehicles. What an awesome victory to witness! It was a very graphic and powerful lesson on using the word as a weapon of warfare, and it is one I have never forgotten.

I have honed and sharpened my warfare over the years. As I write this, it has been seven years since I moved to South Carolina, and the neighbors are still there. I am confident, however, that God will remove them at the appointed time. I have, over and over again, claimed their land for the Kingdom of God.

The lesson in all this is that we have to be very careful and proactive to not allow offense and anger to gain a foothold in our thoughts. Satan is the prince of the air, and he operates in our thoughts to get us to agree with him. Once we agree, we are sucked in. Ephesians 4:26-27 (AMP): "Be angry (at sin—at immorality, at injustice, at ungodly behavior), yet do not sin; do not let your anger last until the sun goes down. And do not give the devil an opportunity (to lead you into sin by holding a grudge, or nurturing anger, or harboring resentment, or cultivating bitterness)."

All sin leads to sickness in one form or another in the human body. Romans 6:23 (NIV) states, "For the wages of sin is death." It was Lucifer who rebelled against

God and brought sin into this world. Adam and Eve just agreed with him and brought sin into mankind. Remember the serpent was in the garden Genesis 3 (AMP): "Now the serpent was more subtle and crafty than any living creature of the field which the Lord God had made. And he (Satan) said to the woman, can it really be that God has said, You shall not eat from every tree of the garden?" Satan always questions God's authority and tries to get you to break every commandment He has said. Once you agree, sin will enter.

Let's say you go to the doctor and he tells you that you have some named disease. Will you agree with that? Or will you rebuke that word and stand on *the Word*? It is not found in the Bible that God gives you disease; it is the sin of this world that has gotten into your thinking and down into the body. The disease does not line up with the promises of God. You need to confess His promises, not keep speaking about your illness. Get out of agreement with the father of lies and into an agreement with God's Word.

It is so funny God's timing of events. I had just finished that last paragraph and closed my laptop to go into town to have a pedicure at my friend Frankie's place. We were talking, and the subject of healing came up and why some people do not get healed, and others have miraculous healings. I said, "Oh my gosh, Frankie, I need to put your testimony in my book." She said,

"Yes, you do, and maybe that's what you came here for today."

Frankie's Testimony

Frankie was diagnosed with breast cancer about eleven years ago. Not just any cancer but the most aggressive type there is. Her response after leaving the doctor's office was to turn to her husband and say, "I do not have cancer, and we will never talk about this again." Instead, she sought the Lord, day and night, read the promises of God, and stood on His word. Her prayer was, *Lord, change the diagnosis.* Her type of cancer, which was the size of a grapefruit, was inoperable. She would not take chemotherapy or radiation; instead, she opted to change her diet and use Essiac tea plus other supplements. Her faithfulness was rewarded with a visit from Jesus, who told her to place her hands on the holes in His hands and her feet on the nail holes in His feet. He said that He took this disease on the cross, and to have faith, He would heal her. In a slow but steady process, the tumor began to shrink. When she went for a PET scan, incredulously, her diagnosis changed. Yes, changed, even after her doctor told her repeatedly that this type of diagnosis does not change. Her tumor went from an aggressive carcinoma to a nonaggressive, operable sarcoma. She had it removed with no other treatment and is cancer-free today.

It is an awesome example of not accepting what is spoken over you if it does not agree with the Word. God honored her faith.

I also have a customer who had cancer in the past and refused chemotherapy, but she did have a hysterectomy. Cancer returned in the lining of her abdomen. She is a great woman of faith and sought the Lord about what to do. She felt led to do the chemotherapy, and I helped her with diet and herbs. She also came in for prayer once a week. We worked on healing the rejection and disappointment in her past. I am happy to say she is cancer-free. She also rejected the diagnosis and spoke God's Word over her life. I think we can never limit how God will heal, for His ways are not our ways. He can use any way to bring healing according to a person's belief and convictions.

Next Level Assignment

In being obedient and coming to South Carolina, I have received some of the most intense training on the Spiritual Gifts that God has given each and every one of us. When we first got here, the only homeschool group I could find for my girls was located at Morningstar Church. My family ended up attending Morningstar for a year, and I went to many prophetic conferences and gatherings over the next few years. Unfortunately, the distance was a problem, and eventually, we decided to look for a church closer to home.

There was this one little church that always caught my eye every time I went to town. My husband and I decided to visit this little church. I have to say that I was not impressed with the first visit. I did not feel the spirit and wanted to go elsewhere, and so we did. But that little church continued to call, and so a year later, we left the other Pentecostal church and returned to Cornerstone Family Worship. It was here I received training in the gifts of Prophecy, Healing, and Deliverance that God desired me to have. These are the gifts of the Holy Spirit, along with the gift of knowledge, that operates in me. Sadly, the majority of the churches do not bother to find out what gifts are in each individual or offer classes or teachings on how to move in your particular gift. We are to be the church: to heal the sick, cast out demons, and raise the dead. You have to practice doing this over and over. Your faith must be exercised, and you have to learn to persevere in the face of disappointment, fear of man, and unbelief. Churches need to be training grounds where people can practice their particular gifts.

I praise my little church and our Pastor, who just wants the manifestation of the Holy Spirit. Here we are free to give prophecy, words of knowledge, lay hands on the sick, and speak in tongues with the interpretation of tongues. It is a church that practices the gifts, a place where we are safe, knowing we are always in training and there is no spirit that demands perfection, and the religious spirit is slowly but surely getting slain by the Holy Spirit. There is no perfect church, but there are churches willing to let the Holy Spirit lead, however that may look.

I had been operating my Naturopathic and Herbal practice out of my home in the country. I was comfort-

able, and my advertising was solely by word of mouth—
I had a pretty good track record with restoring people
to health, praying for them, and seeing them set free.
There were many times I would ask God what the next
step was and where I was going with all this. All he
would say was to be patient and wait on Him. I do not
know about you, but when he says that, I just want to
scream. I am one of those high-energy, can't-sit-down
type of people; I want action.

Nevertheless, I continued my practice, always pressing in for more and more revelation. Here are a few of
the highlights from those years.

I recall one girl who came because she was suffer-
ing from panic attacks. This was a Christian family that
brought their daughter, and I had homeschooled with
them in the past. When I talked with the daughter, I
knew that this was a spirit of fear, and so I rebuked
the spirit and commanded it to leave. Not three minutes later, she starts shaking with a panic attack, and
again I rebuked the spirit, and it left just as suddenly
as it came. I reminded her that she needed to speak the
Word over the spirit of fear, such as, "We have not been
given a Spirit of fear, but of power, love, and a sound
mind" (rephrase of 2 Timothy 1:7). I also gave her herbs
to address the stress on the adrenals and herbs to feed
and calm the nerves. I felt confident that victory had
been won.

Well, it was not! She ended up having such a violent attack that she had to go to the ER, not once but twice. The parents brought her back, and I felt led by the Holy Spirit to try some Sozo or Theophostic prayer ministry. First, we prayed for the Holy Spirit to come and surround us, and then I asked her to bring to mind a personal encounter she had had with Jesus. When she had him in her mind, I asked her what memory immediately came to her when I mentioned the panic attacks. She then isolated a single instance in her memory when she felt fear. I asked her where Jesus was in this memory. It took a few moments, but she told me Jesus was there holding her. She and her sister, who had come with her, burst into happy tears. She told me she felt it leave, and she felt free. She has never, to this day, had another attack. Only Jesus can deliver like this.

There was another woman who brought her teenage daughter. This high school girl was exhausted all the time and had developed some nervous tics. When speaking with her, I discerned the spirit of fear (fear of her peers and fear of what people think of her), along with the taint of the occult. I am pretty bold, and I just pray what the Holy Spirit shows me. I bound the spirit of fear and the spirit of witchcraft and broke their power over her life. The mother and daughter were Christians, so I told them she needed to speak the word over this to get her victory. I gave her an adrenal formula and an herbal formula to calm the nerves and sent them on their way.

I did not hear from the mother for a year when she called and said she needed to bring her daughter back in. When they arrived, the mother told me that the difference last time was immediate. She said her daughter had stopped compulsively spinning and touching the ground. This was the spirit of witchcraft which she was delivered from, but apparently, that and the spirit of fear were back. It is difficult sometimes to get people totally set free. They have to stand firm in the Word of God, and there are many who are not willing to do the warfare. Remember what Peter said, "Be alert and of sober mind. Your enemy the devil prowls around like a roaring lion looking for someone to devour. Resist him, standing firm in the faith" (1 Peter 5:8-9 NIV). It is a continual battle for our souls, day in and day out.

I once again helped this young woman, and once again, she was set free.

It was during the pandemic of 2020, in the month of April, right after the lockdown began, that the Lord spoke to me very clearly one morning. He told me to go to town, rent the building I had looked at some months ago, operate my business from there, and open up a public Healing Room.

Back in January, my friend Cynthia and I had discussed going into business together. We had gone into town and walked up and down the main street looking at rentals, but nothing seemed right. We drove over to the next street, and there was a single stand-alone brick building for rent. It has a beautiful wrought iron gate around it, and when I opened the gate, I heard that very small voice say, "this is it." We called the realtor, and she came right over and showed us the place. Old oak floors and high ceilings with crown molding graced the rooms, and it had a kitchen and two bathrooms. We loved it but did not know how we were going to swing the rent. We left it up to God to tell us what He wanted to do. Cynthia then ended up having to care for her grandchildren during the day, so she was unable to commit to anything then.

So, when God spoke, I knew exactly what building He was talking about. The Lord had spoken some time ago to Brenda at my church that she was to form a healing team. There were five of us on that team at the beginning of the year, and we knew God was going to call two more to make it a team of seven women. I texted everyone on the team, and we all agreed to meet the owner of the building the next day. Incredibly, everyone on that team seemed to have doubts about using the building. It was too small, it was this, it was that. I ended up feeling like I got the word from the Lord wrong. I called Brenda, and we decided to look at other buildings, but nothing fit what I needed for my practice. I felt increasingly agitated and moody, and I could not figure out what I was supposed to do.

I went home frustrated and told my husband everything that was transpiring. I will never forget when he jokingly said, "What do you expect with a group of women? Nobody is going to agree on the same thing." Boom. The Holy Spirit hit me! Immediately a scripture popped into my mind; Romans 8:5 (NIV): "Those who live according to the sinful nature have their minds set on what that nature desires; but those who live in accordance with the Spirit have their minds set on what the Spirit desires." Good golly, I was listening to all the women but not to what the Holy Spirit had told me!

The next day I called the woman who owned the building and told her I wanted to sign the lease that day. I could not do this soon enough, as the conviction by the Holy Spirit was very strong. As soon as I had secured the lease, I experienced total peace. I called the healing team after the fact, telling them I had signed the lease and how very strongly the Holy Spirit had dealt with the decisions I was making. Everyone suddenly was in total agreement. How interesting.

I opened my shop in mid-June. Cynthia did join me for a while but left to care for her aging mother. On Thursday evenings, we open the doors to the public for healing ministry. At the onset, it has been a huge success. People come far and wide to receive prayer. A few of our ladies attend Global Awakenings School of Healing, and we are in the process of looking into registering with the International Healing Rooms. For now, we are covered by, and we are an extension of my church, Cornerstone Family Worship. We flow well together, all seven of us, and the Lord is doing a work in this season to prepare us for the greater works. We have no doubt this little building will rock this small town with the power of the Holy Spirit. Several of us have had dreams and visions of people lined up for healing. Visions of tents set up in the parking lot and signs, miracles, and wonders abounding. We are in the process.

We have had some great testimonies in these few short months. One woman came in completely wasted in the flesh. She was under the care of a naturopath, but she was unable to gain any weight and continued to diminish. We began to pray for healing and then realized the prayers were not being received. After some probing, we saw that there was a lot of unforgiveness. We had her offer up to Jesus everyone she had not forgiven, and she then repented of holding onto bitterness. There were also spirits of rejection we had her pray to release.

Often, we get the person to repeat the prayers after us so that they are actively participating in their healing. I tell you: you could feel those spirits leave her; it was a powerful release. It was reported by her mother the following week that she had begun to steadily gain weight after that night. Unforgiveness and bitterness will literally eat you up inside!

A woman in her thirties came with stage 4 kidney failure. After much coaching about diet (fast food was a major problem), we got down to prayer. This woman also had much unforgiveness towards her mother and various family members. The spirit of rejection was also addressed, along with the spirit of bitterness that arises out of rejection. After a long prayer session, she left feeling loads lighter. I had given her herbs for cleaning the debris out of the kidneys coupled with bowel and liver cleansing herbs, plus a good sea vegetable combination. Two days later, I received this email:

Good evening, Wendy,

I have a praise report! I had bloodwork scheduled for Friday (I saw you Wednesday evening and began treatment that night.) My GFR range the Nephrologist set based on my history was 30–40 percent, July 1. On August 1, my GFR was 44 percent. My GFR on Friday, 9/4, was 62 percent! My Creatinine was 1.61 in February this year. It was 1.39 last month, 8/4, and *praise God*, Friday it was 1.04! I went from 1 point from being stage 4 to stage 2.

Now that is nothing but a miracle from God! How awesome are His healing powers! Healing is much more rapid when the spiritual sickness is addressed. If we were more spiritually aware on this planet, we would look to the spirit first and then work our way down to the body. As the word says, "Every good thing given and every perfect gift is from above; coming down from the Father of lights, with whom there is no variation or shifting shadow" (James 1:17 NASB).

A busy work-from-home mother of four children came to me, desperate for help. She was tired and angry, her periods put her in a horrible mood, and she was snappy to her children. She felt like she had all this anger and confusion in her mind. After my initial intake process, we focused on her abandonment in childhood by a parent and the feelings that arose out of there. Unforgiveness toward the parent was renounced, along with the feelings of abandonment and rejection. Then we renounced the spirit of bitterness and all seven underling spirits and broke their power in her life. In addition, I addressed her hormones with an herbal glandular tonic and an adrenal formula, and I fed her overstressed nerves with an herbal nerve repair recipe. She emailed me the next day saying she felt much lighter and had a sense of peace and calm that she had never felt. She also stated that our prayer session was much more powerful than anything she had ever experienced in church.

I know we are coming to a time and a season where miracles will be commonplace. God is going to raise his Body of Believers to a higher level. One day we will understand that our spirit bodies must be in alignment with His word and divine plan to achieve perfect health. This would result in taking better care of our food and environment; it is an all-encompassing work. To be in perfect health, the Trinity must be involved: "And the very God of peace sanctify you wholly; and *I pray God* your whole spirit and soul and body be preserved blameless unto the coming of our Lord Jesus Christ" (1 Thessalonians 5:23 KJB). May we truly be the sons and daughters of the God Most High that we were created to be.

Until that time, I will continually persevere, pressing into God and His word to understand where the sickness lies, laying hands on the sick, proclaiming their healing in the name of Jesus, casting out demons, and teaching and training people on food and herbs to achieve the vibrant health we have been promised. We are all a work in progress, and we must daily put down the life of the flesh and raise up the life in the spirit.

CPSIA information can be obtained
at www.ICGtesting.com
Printed in the USA
LVHW081151280623
750574LV00004B/106